D1568776

Matters of Fact

Matters of Fact

A sociological inquiry

Stanley Raffel
Department of Sociology
University of Edinburgh

Routledge & Kegan Paul
London, Boston and Henley

First published in 1979
by Routledge & Kegan Paul Ltd
39 Store Street, London WC1E 7DD,
Broadway House, Newtown Road,
Henley-on-Thames, Oxon RG9 1EN and
9 Park Street, Boston, Mass. 02108, USA
Set in Palatino by
Bishopsgate Press Ltd
and printed in Great Britain by
Redwood Burn Ltd
Trowbridge and Esher

British Library Cataloguing in Publication Data

Raffel, Stanley
Matters of fact.
1. Records – Social aspects 2. Knowledge, Sociology of
I. Title
301.14   HM73   78–40800

ISBN 0–7100–0034–0

Contents

Acknowledgments   vii

Part One   **The Grounds of the Activity of Recording**   **1**

  1   Introduction   3
  2   Observations and records   21
  3   Records and events   48

Part Two   **Implications of the Grounds of Records for the Uses of Records**   **75**

  4   Reliability   77
  5   Completeness   102

     Notes   117

v

Acknowledgments

In 1965, I was fortunate enough to meet two people who were willing to teach me, Peter McHugh and Alan Blum. The various results, practical and theoretical, of my on-going relationship with them are too diverse to acknowledge here. However, I can and should record some of the high points in the story of how this particular work is indebted to them.

Blum first suggested that I study records. Furthermore, as he has done repeatedly in similar situations since, he was willing to devote his energy and creativity to the mundane task of finding a way where none seemed to exist for me to pursue my studies. My efforts to look at records in terms of their idea began with a devastating but (typically) totally honest critique McHugh made of my first attempt to write about records. Later, when a draft was in deep intellectual and administrative trouble, they undertook a major and time-consuming salvage operation, providing me with fresh ideas for a reformulation, help with the writing, and principled advice for overcoming the administrative hurdles. Still later, when there was yet another crisis, this time over publication, they intervened with ideas not just for overcoming publishers' reservations, but at the same time making the work a truer statement of what I wanted to say.

Elaine Samuel has helped me to develop many of the ideas reported here. In addition, she has edited at least three drafts with understanding, intelligence, and even affection.

Life in Edinburgh was made lively and rewarding largely through associations with a few gifted students, Patrick Colfer, James Stewart, Colin May, Mick Campion, and Janet Parry. Ideas generated in innumerable conversations with them have found their way into this manuscript.

Gianfranco Poggi has read two previous drafts very carefully. I must also thank him for providing important practical support just when it was needed.

The hospital data were collected while I was a project supervisor on a medical research project headed by Elliot Freidson, with the assistance of Derek Phillips.

Note: 'Mont Royal' is a cover name for the hospital.

Part One

The Grounds of the Activity of Recording

1 Introduction

The work reported here, begun as a study of medical records in a large, modern hospital, has broadened into an attempt to formulate the nature of records. The hospital studied is typical of modern hospitals in having an abundance of medical records. There are daily notes by doctors and nurses concerning the health of all patients, past and present. These make up the bulk of what hospital personnel call the 'medical record'. In addition, there is a plethora of records recording most of the important events in a patient's hospital career. Long notes reporting on admission and discharge are entered into the 'record' by doctors. When the patient is admitted, he is supposed to have an extensive physical examination, which is duly described for the record, as are any operations the patient may have. Pathologists, social workers, and psychiatrists enter reports of examinations. If a patient dies, that too will be described in detail for the record. If discharged patients are seen in out-patients' clinics, reports on these examinations are entered as well. In this study, when we refer to records, it is these medical records which furnish most of our concrete examples. However, as the most distinctive feature of this work is not the subject matter but the way we have decided to approach it, it is necessary to say how we intend to analyse records. The discussion is meant to apply to records in general rather than specifically to medical records.

Instead of beginning with a definition of records, we shall begin with a discussion of what has been said to justify records for sociological use. These justifications turn primarily upon an unstated notion of fact as a relation between record and event, which parallels the idea of language as a relation of words to things. Our concept of what records *are* will emerge as we consider the idea of a record which is implicit in historical and sociological discussions of records.

3

Sociologists and historians use records as data which permit them to infer 'what has happened'. Records are, of course, the historian's major source of data. Collingwood describes history as follows:[1]

> History proceeds by the interpretation of evidence: where evidence is a collective name for things which singly are called documents and a document is a thing existing here and now, of such a kind that the historian, by thinking about it, can get answers to the questions he asks about past events.

Kitson Clark writes that 'Documents in official archives are necessarily one of the main . . . sources of information for the historian.'[2] Gottschalk writes:[3]

> The history of historians is two things: (a) a process of examining records and survivals, and, (b) a way of 'writing up' or otherwise presenting the results of that examination.

Records are used by historians to get 'as close to what actually happened as we can . . . from a critical examination of the best available sources.'[4]

An interesting point is being asserted but not explicated in these quotations: the facts are not the records themselves, but that which the records report, which is to say there is an implicit suggestion here of some unexplicated relation between the record and the event reported by the record. Collingwood, for example, by asking us to 'think about' records in order to learn about events is proposing a relation between record and event. However, as an explication of the relation, 'think about' is, of course, too vague. In thinking about records one is apparently somehow able to move from thinking about the record to thinking about what the record is 'about'. Although the record is in one sense a thing to be thought about it is also a special kind of thing, a thing which can be related to other things so as to be 'about' them. Gottschalk, by proposing that records can get us 'close to what actually happened', is proposing some such record-event relationship. The record is not what happened but can (somehow) get us near to what happened. We shall not object to Gottschalk's or Collingwood's

4

proposals but we shall explicate the record-event relationship which they assert.

That we can consider Gottschalk's and Collingwood's speech an assertion but not an explication is itself worth consideration. How did they come to fail in this way and what does their failure teach? Assertions resonate with security, with certainty, with being definite. Originally, 'to assert' designated 'to join to'. Their speech, then, is another instance of the idea of a record – certain because it is joined to (about, close to) something other than itself, either the event or in their case the idea of a record. Their certainty comes from their own lack of originality. The copy knows how it was produced because it can point to externals as its source. The copy, then, tries to avoid starting by externalizing its start.

The deeper issue, though, is why the copy is afraid to experience its own start. It thinks what starts determines what comes after in just the way it is determined (it can only follow) the event. The copy is afraid to start because, by starting, it would be determining everything. This is too much for any man – totally determining is God's work – so the copy naturally prefers to be totally determined, i.e., to let someone else start. Gottschalk and Collingwood might hear the request for explication (for thought about the source of their speech) as irresponsibly asking *them* to start. They would responsibly plead ignorance (the other side of their certainty) by pointing to the mystery of the original event or record as what made their speeches necessary. Their mistake is that asking them to explicate is not asking them to determine everything. It is not a request that they start again, produce rather than reproduce, but that they accept the fact that they have started (to speak about records). Having started they need an end, a ground, a reason, an explanation of what they are doing. One who is willing to explicate, then, counters the record not with a new start but through facing the fact that a start is not an end.

Although sociologists are less likely than historians to make use of records, many sociological studies, both classic and modern, have made extensive use of them. The original sources of Emile Durkheim's statistical data in *Suicide* were presumably written records.[5] In *The Polish Peasant in Europe and America*, William Thomas and Florian Znaniecki used various types of records, including but by no means only 'first person' accounts. They also used court records, the records of legal aid societies, coroners' records, and the case records of a charitable organization.[6] In the famous Hawthorne studies, Roethlisberger and Dickson relied on written records for some of their data. They offered this account of the usefulness of 'daily historical records':[7]

> This [the record] was designed to give a complete account of the daily happenings in the test room: what changes were introduced, the remarks made by operators . . . the daily problems with which the investigators were concerned, and all other observations that might be of value in interpreting the output curve. . . . This record was invaluable in reconstructing the history of the test room.

Like historians, then, sociologists are using records in order to determine 'what happened', and like historians they are therefore relying on a relationship between record and event without explicating it.

Among the many kinds of records used in more modern studies have been Navy records in an investigation of the causes of airplane accidents,[8] plant records in an investigation of worker morale,[9] medical records in a study of imaginary insect bites,[10] and court records in an analysis of delinquency rates in the USSR.[11]

While noting that records are but one of the many possible data sources for sociologists, methodologists often recommend that records be used in sociological research. Riley suggests that certain types of records make available facts which cannot be obtained by most research methods:[12]

> Medical, psychoanalytic, or social-work case records . . . may serve as 'expert' records of complex human relationships and processes, affording insights not open to the lay investigator who himself attempts to gather such technical material.

Moreover:

> Available data can be used as the basis for research on interaction – and on the very type of continuing private interaction that is usually inaccessible to direct observation.

Selltiz also notes some of the advantages researchers can gain by using records.[13]

> [Records] . . . have a number of advantages in social
> research, in addition to that of economy. A major one is the
> fact that much information is collected periodically, thus
> making possible the establishment of trends over time.
> Another is that the gathering of information from such
> sources does not require the cooperation of the individuals
> about whom the information is being sought, as does the
> use of questionnaires, interviews, projective techniques and,
> frequently, observation.

Although Riley and Selltiz are more interested in discussing the advantages involved in the use of particular kinds of records than in outlining general features of all records, more issues concerning the record-event relationship are implicit in what they say. Riley's second point assumes that a record (at least from the viewpoint of the researcher to whom it is 'available') is not direct observation. She is pointing to (but not explicating) a feature of records, namely, that in looking at a record one is indirectly looking at some other thing, in this case private interaction. But how does a record make such interaction accessible? Why is the record best seen not as a thing which is itself accessible but as a thing which makes other things accessible? Selltiz tells us that periodic collection makes it possible to establish a trend over time. Presumably the existence of more than one record (through periodic collection) is not the trend over time which Selltiz has in mind. In some unexplicated way, what is important about the recorded information is not that it is itself in time (even though it is periodically collected) but that it can tell us about other things which may form trends over time. The record, in that it permits us to 'establish' things, is somehow outside time (eternal?) and yet it can tell us about other things (events?) which are in time.

Selltiz also notes that gathering information from records does not require the co-operation of the record's subjects. The absence of the need for co-operation amounts to another implicit statement concerning the record-event relationship. Co-operation is not required in that the record-event relationship is not between one speaker and another (who would have to co-operate) but between a speech (record) and what the speech is supposed to reveal (the event). How has the record made the subjects of the record, even if they are persons, into things which reveal themselves to readers of the record, whether the subjects like it or not?

Riley and Selltiz could 'answer' these various questions but their answers would do precisely what records themselves do, namely point, in their case, to advantages of records. What reasoning leads them to answer with points? If the start is the end, in order to proceed Riley and Selltiz need only follow the path laid down by records. Basically, they proceed without asking any questions. What will they make of a question? A questioner must have lost sight of the start, i.e., of the unquestionable, because original good of the event. Our problem (question) is that we are lost. Their solution (answer) gets us back on the track by pointing to the starting point: the unquestioned value of the event and the subsidiary value of the record which will lead us to it. Their answer reaffirms their sense of how they started, i.e., by being pointed in the right direction by the event. A questioner who is *not* lost, e.g., one who asks why a record should not be seen as itself accessible begins to look irresponsible in the sense of unwilling to follow the path of the event and so presumably following his own path. However Riley has misunderstood this question. It comes not out of a desire to begin anew but to find the end (reason) and not just the beginning of her pointing. The question suggests that by pointing Riley has made a difference between a start and an end, namely the difference between originating as events do and desiring to return to the path in the way a lost person who follows Riley's advice does. Pointing, just like copying, has responsibility because its so-called externals cannot account for its need to be itself.

Reading records may not require co-operation but surely reading records and writing records involve *some* kinds of operations whose rules of procedure deserve to be specified. Selltiz and Riley do not try to explicate the characteristics of records or describe how they are produced and read. Other writers have focused on the disadvantages of records but we shall find that they are no closer than Riley and Selltiz to a consideration of the issues we wish to discuss.

Disadvantages involved in the use of records are as common a theme in the literature as advantages. Many writers have warned of the danger of 'bias' in records. In his discussion of documents, Cicourel writes:[14]

> Historical and contemporary non-scientific materials contain built-in biases and the researcher generally has no access to the setting in which they were produced; the meanings intended by the producer of a document and the cultural circumstances surrounding its assembly are not always subject to manipulation and control.

and Douglas warns:[15]

> the official statistics on suicide are probably biased in a number of ways . . . such that the various sociological theories of suicide will be unreliably supported by these official statistics.

Sjoberg and Nett alert us to sources of bias in the records of government officials [16] and newsmen.[17]

Bias, of course, is not just the simple matter of outright dishonesty. As most writers on the topic see it, there are also more subtle dangers inherent in the use of records than the possibility that the records are blatantly dishonest. Even relatively honest records may present only a one-sided view of the events they purport to describe. Cochran has warned of the danger of subscribing to records which present a sentimental version of reality:[18]

> By taking the written record that was easiest to use and the most stirring from a sentimental or romantic stand-point, that is, the record of the Federal Government, the American historian prepared the way for one of the major misconceptions in American [history] . . . the primary role of the central government in our historical development.

Goode suggests why lower-class persons may be underrepresented in written records, thus leading to incomplete pictures of the past:[19]

> So high a percentage of past populations were made up of people with odd histories. A high percentage were illiterate

and in any event not important enough to figure in written records, or in the conversations of people who did write diaries, letters, and books.

Furthermore, if one depends upon records for one's knowledge, there will be certain periods about which one cannot know anything at all:[20]

> *A fortiori*, the past of generations long dead, most of whom left no records or whose records, if they exist, have never been disturbed by the historian's touch, is beyond recall in its entirety.

> When literacy is low, not only do fewer people record their private or public thoughts, and create fewer documents . . . but all documents are socially less important in such a period, and thus less likely to survive.[21]

Although there are obvious differences between discussing advantages and discussing disadvantages of records, both kinds of discussion do have at least one thing in common. In both cases, the record-event link is being assumed rather than explicated. That the many methodological difficulties just mentioned have to be dealt with at all suggests that there is a contingent relation between any record and what the record is meant to do, namely reveal facts. Perhaps this point seems obvious, but it is odd that the standard in accordance with which the relation comes to be contingent remains both unexamined and unformulated. From Goode's, Gottschalk's, and Cochran's accounts, for example, we may gather the following: events may or may not have records; events without records cannot be known; some records of events fail to be good records. Again we have the assertion of a relationship between record and event and we have this relationship as a contingency. Still missing is an explication of what exactly the relationship is, how it has come about, and why it is a contingent relationship. Thus Goode relies on the fact that records must 'survive' but does not tell us why they must. What, to take just one of many possible questions we could address to his account, is the difference between event and record such that events do not have to survive and records do? Is the record a substitute for the event, the survival of the record somehow ensuring the survival of the event? Perhaps this formulation is correct but if so we have additional interesting issues to address. What kind of thing *can* adequately substitute for another thing given that some things (including some records) can be poor substitutes? What features of events make substitution necessary and what features of records make substitution possible? Furthermore, if some records can fail to be good substitutes, by what standard do we differentiate good from bad substitutes?

Goode's reliance on the need for survival brings the central issues to the fore again. If the start determines everything, the start cannot have an end since that would reintroduce the indeterminacy that the start supposedly remedied. Death loses its place within life as the end of the start that is birth and becomes a problem to be remedied through records ensuring survival. Questioning Goode's need for survival would appear to him as the irresponsible rejection of life. Since the start determines everything, questioning the start is proposing a new one. Starting with a question rather than an answer would be starting negatively instead of positively, i.e., starting with death rather than life. How else to hear the request for an explanation of the need for survival besides as a death wish? Following Goode's example of the lower classes and past generations, survival is not inevitable or natural for man since it comes only from the unnatural record or unnatural suggestion by Goode. Man will not survive naturally but only if he knows what is good for him. Our questions are not meant to recommend the unnatural (death) but to suggest to Goode and the rest that their speech does not naturally follow from the existence of the event. It therefore is not endless but has, like life, a beginning (the fact that events die and records can be preserved) and an end (the authors' desire to preserve events). These authors are alive and not just surviving in the way a recorded event survives and so they can answer questions by authoritatively saying why they act, even if it is only keeping records. Questions are not meant to tempt them not to exist but to show them they are responsible for the way they exist.

One way to inspect the opinions of sociologists and historians about records is to distinguish between those who think records provide relatively good data and those who think records provide relatively bad data. At one extreme, Garfinkel can argue that records are almost always bad data:[22]

> Any investigator who has attempted a study with the use of clinic records, almost wherever such records are found, has his litany of troubles to recite. Moreover, hospital and clinic administrators frequently are as knowledgeable and concerned about these 'shortcomings' as are the investigators themselves.

At the other extreme, Shera can state that:[23]

> The official public records of highly civilized countries probably more nearly approach perfect evidence than any other form of documentation.

In between are many methodologically inclined sociologists and historians who have discussed the dangers inherent in the use of records and, also, methods for reducing the dangers. A general theme of most discussions is that there are both advantages and disadvantages in the use of records as data. Whichever side is taken, however, the important point for us remains the existence of an implicit standard to which we must refer in order to decide whether a given record or all records are factual. Both sides are relying on something while failing to talk about it. They are relying on conceptions of what makes the record good, of what makes the record factual. Therefore, we shall be discussing the deeper issue, namely the *possibility* of making the claim that records are factual, whether or not that claim is rejected in any given empirical case.

Researchers who use records in their studies and methodologists who discuss problems inherent in records share a basic commitment to conceiving of records as sources of data, however inadequate, which permit inferences, albeit not certainty, about the real world. In terms of this interest methodological discussions concerning records are inadequate because they beg our question: they presuppose the grounds which make it possible that records *could* be facts and investigate, instead, whether given records *are* facts. For example, in his supposedly thorough discussion, Gottschalk offers rules for deciding whether records are truthful:[24]

(1) Because reliability is, in general, inversely proportional to the time-lapse between event and recollection, the closer the document is to the event it narrates the better it is likely to be for historical purposes. (2) Because documents differ in purpose . . . the more serious the author's intention to make a mere record, the more dependable his document as a historical source. . . . (3) Because the testimony of a schooled or experienced observer and reporter . . . is generally superior to that of the untrained and casual observer and reporter, the greater the expertness of the author in the matter he is reporting, the more reliable his report.

Gottschalk also notes that 'official histories must be treated with caution'[25] and that 'there are laws and conventions which oblige witnesses to depart from strict veracity.'[26]

Gottschalk sees these rules as principles to be followed by competent researchers. For us, the very existence of these rules generates questions. Why is reliability always a trouble in research based on records?[27] What is the connection between records and recollection?[28] What is the connection between records and events?[29] Why does the character of observers always become an issue in research using records?[30] What is the relationship of records to the ideal of 'veracity'?[31]

More basically, what is the nature of records such that Gottschalk and others must formulate rules about their use, and what are records such that these particular rules might seem reasonable? In other words, we neither accept nor reject Gottschalk's rules. Instead, we want to understand the grounds which make these rules seem necessary and reasonable. Reliability, for example, is associated with time for Gottschalk. What socially enforced idea of time does Gottschalk conceal ('time-lapse' is cryptic to say the least) which makes it possible to be 'close' in time and which enables this kind of temporal access to be more adequate for truth than distance? We need a rendering of the standard normative order of social science which methodically selects and distinguishes truth-producing scientific recording, apparently on the basis of presence and absence.

In rule 2 above, Gottschalk asks that the authors seriously

intend to make a record. The notion of seriousness here creates more problems than it solves. We can, for example, treat with suspicion any author who seriously intends to make a record, there being all sorts of bureaucratic and political records felt to be untrustworthy for this very reason. Think of the difference in this case between 'he intended to make the record' in Gottschalk's sense, whatever that is, and 'he deliberately set out to make that record'. What do we presuppose of the serious author who intends to make a record, then, distinguished from the one who deliberately makes the one he does; and why is the one who is not serious less likely to produce a truthful record, given that Gottschalk probably wants us to be disinterested rather than politicized and the casual recorder might be the most disinterested of all?

Continuing on to the schooled observer, as distinct from the casual reporter, we might ask what Gottschalk expects from the former. Perhaps he is expert, in the sense that the historian could read the document with the understanding that it had been written with his historian's standards in mind, that it was written by someone of whom it could be said that he knew what he was doing – he is history's representative in so far as the historian/reader can ignore temporal distance through a surrogate presence.

Gottschalk admits that these rules are not hard and fast. Others can argue, for example, that official histories make the *best* records,[32] or that nearness to the event can lead to bias.[33] Therefore we can also ask: What is the nature of records such that Gottschalk's rules need not apply, such that closeness to an event can sometimes be a hindrance and official histories can be the most informative records? And, more basically, is there a rule or better a principle which would make necessary both Gottschalk's rules and the exceptions to them. We suspect that there is and, furthermore, that Gottschalk is relying on it in making his definite assertions about records.

The rules are not hard and fast in that they assert what is only likely to be the case. Like a statistician, Gottschalk speaks of probabilities rather than certainties. How does the fact that he speaks in this way square with our earlier notion that record-writers and writers about record-writers obtain certainty by copying events? Gottschalk has the natural urge of a speaker to generalize. But how can he unify two (records) when the two, *qua* two, are different? The solution is the self-same one that permits the record-writer, who is after all different from the event, to speak of it. Two records may be different but they may also resemble each other. Gottschalk will address only what they have in common. Gottschalk's topic becomes the likely, i.e., the ways in which things are alike. The problem remains of what to do with the unlikely. The unlikely gets reconceived as the exception, which is to say it is excepted from speech. So Gottschalk might understand the queries about his exceptions as the eccentric refusal to go along with the majority, or the tyrannical desire for rule of the few (unlikely) over the many (likely), or as sheer refusal to speak (generalize). Yet we want neither to tyrannize Gottschalk nor to have no rule at all. By seeing the place of his exceptions, Gottschalk could see how his propositions are rooted not in a *rule*, e.g., that we should get close to the event, but in a *principle*, i.e., that we should be alike rather than unlike. The exceptional is certainly not an exception to this principle since the very need to formulate it depends on the existence of exceptions. The exception is *Gottschalk's* real topic in that it provides his whole reason for having to speak. Really, we are asking Gottschalk for the good of being alike. And his answer, which takes the form of fearing the question, is that by being alike he avoids having to go first, i.e., having to rule. He thinks he is not ruling because he lets the majority rule. However, if only by letting the majority rule, he *is* beginning in the sense of having a principle. One with principles, unlike one with rules, need not be a tyrant even if he starts because his start demands not obedience but dialogue. By considering his exceptions, Gottschalk would not be submitting but coming to grips with his principles.

We have already noticed, along with Gottschalk, that records may or may not be adequate. Gottschalk is interested in poor records as poor history, of course, in that inadequate records become a feature of inadequate historians, that inadequate recorders become features of inadequate records that become features of inadequate historians – i.e., the collector is a feature of that which he collects. So Gottschalk must provide (tacitly) for differentiating his collection from the problematic status which he concedes attends any historico-sociological research even when that research follows his rules. Gottschalk can formulate his own history as an instance of good history through some (unexamined) characterization of the record as requiring presence and disinterest. The observer, he tells us, must have a particular relation to time (presence) and must produce in himself a particular orientation (disinterest). But Gottschalk never questions the *reason* for collecting in the first place. If he did he might be able to formulate the idea which generates both the adequate and the inadequate and thus could be relieved of the stipulation that his rules are themselves inadequate to a defence of the adequate record. We shall try to find the principles that provide for both Gottschalk's rules and the exceptions to them.

Even the work of ethnomethodologists is inadequate to us unless it can be redirected to the grounds of the activity of recording. Blum and McHugh's description of ethnomethodology makes the relevant point in another context:[34]

> Ethnomethodology seeks to 'rigorously describe' ordinary usage, and despite its significant transformation of standards for conceiving of and describing such usage, it still conducts its enquiries under the auspices of a concrete, positivistic conception of adequacy. Ethnomethodology conceives of such descriptions of usage as analytic 'solutions' to their tasks, whereas our interest is in the production of the idea which makes any conception of relevant usage itself possible.

Although Garfinkel has described some 'troubles' associated with the use of records and some 'good organizational reasons' for these troubles,[35] he has not yet explicated the basic idea of records which makes these troubles with records possible. Garfinkel reports 'troubles' for potential users of records, for example, missing information, ambiguous information, irrelevant information. However, by focusing on 'poor' records, he may be misleading. Is it really so obvious how even a good record could 'inform' us? What are people saying when they read a record and say that they 'learned something'? Obviously, 'learning something' or even 'getting information' from a record is a different matter from 'learning something' from a novel, but exactly what is the difference? Garfinkel mentions that good record-writers should 'get the story right'.[36] But what is it about record-writers and records that makes it even possible that they can be 'right' or 'wrong', unlike, for example, novelists, who are evaluated by totally different standards? Furthermore, the easy answers to these questions are themselves questionable. If records can be 'right' or 'wrong' by corresponding to the world or not, how is *that* possible? How can one thing (a record) correspond to another thing (a world)?

Record-writing must depend on some kind of interesting segregating procedure by which two things, a record and the 'world' are, first, differentiated from each other and, then, related to each other so as to make the one, ideally, 'about' the other. But how can one thing be about another? Again, we are back to the idea that records are a special kind of thing, i.e., words, but surely the word-thing relationship exemplified in records needs to be formulated in more detail than just saying it is 'troublesome'. After all, even novels are 'about things' in some sense, so again, what is the difference between a record and a novel? The obvious answer, that records are about the real world whereas novels are about other kinds of things, would not get us too far. If we did try this route toward an answer, surely we would have to provide an adequate formulation of this 'real world' which records are differentiated from and then related to in such a way as to produce an 'about' or 'correspondence' relationship.

There is another problem with Garfinkel's formulation of record-keeping besides the fact that it leaves so many interesting issues unexplicated. Perhaps because he does not see anything worth talking about in the 'obvious' features of records we are going to examine, in order to have news, Garfinkel is forced to exaggerate. In the quotation which we reported earlier, Garfinkel stated that all investigators find records inadequate. Obviously, though, some persons do *not* think they have trouble with records. For Garfinkel these cases are so uninteresting that he chooses to ignore them. However, in terms of the questions we raised about records, those who succeed in using records are as interesting as anyone else. In succeeding they must have solved all the problems we have already raised. For example, they must have somehow been able to see one thing (a record) as both different from and corresponding to another thing (the world). More generally, they must have used some normative order to decide that a given record or all records are 'good'.

In a way, Garfinkel is like Gottschalk in that his description does not cover all the cases. The troublesome character of records is a possibility but not a necessity. Therefore, to describe records as troublesome, as Garfinkel does, is not to make enough progress towards a formulation of the nature of the idea of records. Again, if Garfinkel would address and attempt to formulate the basic conception which allows records to be seen as fact, he might be able to provide both for those who find records troublesome and for those who do not. Both groups presumably have in common some implicit and unexplicated notion of what constitutes a good record. It is this underlying idea that we shall try to get at. We shall come in the end to salvage Garfinkel's notion that *all* records are troublesome but only by realizing that what troubles the investigator is not a contingent feature of some records but the very idea of a record. A record is always some trouble in that records instance the trouble of self-denial, excusing oneself rather than responding. Even a good record will turn out to be mere relief from responsibility and so will trouble the one who knows that relief is not understanding.

In the whole discussion so far, the fact that there is only a contingent relationship between record and event makes reference to the exigency that what a record records (i.e., the 'original' material, the event) is, strictly speaking, unknowable, and so the adequacy of any record is problematic. Certainty is impossible, the only sure thing being that the record exists. What conception orients us to this version of records and thus also provides for the rules of thumb and practical problems we have reviewed?

Although formulating in detail the underlying conception of a record is the major task ahead of us, we can offer some preliminary remarks now. The best record is one that is a photocopy of the event. The record is not supposed to be an independent thing but merely a reflection (copy) of another thing. The record repeats the event but is not supposed to be, in any important sense, itself an event. To understand how a record could be a copy, we must understand how 'fact' (rather than fantasy, humour, etc.) can be seen in the document – how the record can be a possible copy of that which is external to it. Seeing fact-in-a-document requires distinguishing between document and event as a matter of boundaries, limits, the outside (what the record reports), and the inside (the record, the word). The record and its events stand in a relation of asymmetric externality and independence:

(1) The events are not seen as produced by the record, but the record is seen as produced by the events.
(2) The events can occur and remain unrecorded, but the record cannot occur without the events.

In social science any event which goes unrecorded is thought to be real but not to be communal property. The event needs to become socialized – it needs a name, and until it becomes socialized, it has no status as a fact. Having been socialized, it is made accessible as a possible topic. The relation of events to records is a relation of exterior, constraining things to words, which generates the possibility of attention by the social scientist according to his conception of socialized fact. This is why social fact is at the deepest level socialized fact.

By the same token, these relations establish matters of evidence as well as topic. If there is no event corresponding to a record, the record has no author(ity); it lacks status as a namer of anything. The rules of thumb on training and observing which we have reviewed address how we may see fact in a document as a matter of preserving this relation of asymmetric direction between event and word. Gottschalk's description of the recorder amounts to a description of the way the record should be made. That the recorder should be disinterested can now be seen to mean that he should be interested only in that it happened. That is, the record should be a product, not of his interest but of the event. Gottschalk's 'serious' author intending to make a 'mere' record must be an author who is willing to let the event make the record. That the record is merely a record means that the record (or recorder) has not produced the event. A 'mere' record, then, is one that has been produced by nothing but the event it purports to record. The observer's presence in time when the event happens, his 'closeness' to the event must be a device for ensuring that the event will produce a record, i.e., that someone will be able to let his speech amount to nothing but a product of the event, thereby supplying science with a fact to which it can attend.

The way a record is prepared and organized provides for our conception of a photo-copy by detaching the thing (event) from the word (record) in such a way as to make the link of asymmetric direction transparent. The various problems with records (the potential absence of an event corresponding to the record, the failure of an observer to be present, the over-involvement of a recorder in his record, etc.) stem from a version of fact as contingent upon the segregation of thing and word. *Our* problem will be to explicate the rationality of the idea which makes the record possible, the idea that the event but not the word should produce the record.

2 Observations and records

In chapter 1 we noted that words must be segregated from and then made dependent on events if the idea of a record is to be made intelligible. The notion of a record requires that the word can be thought of, not as an event, but as 'about' events. Chapter 2 continues this examination of records by considering how it is possible and why it is rational to bring about the word-thing relationship exemplified in the record. We approach these topics through a consideration of the action necessary to produce a record. Medical records are produced by persons who are supposed to be engaged in the activity which might be called observation.[1] We might feel inclined to say, then, that the factual status of records is established by the fact that they are produced by observers. Although our records are produced by observers, merely to stipulate this point is to say nothing about the factual status of records, because whatever it is that would comprise the action of an adequate observer remains to be specified. If one can produce a good record by being a good observer, then our topics must become what it is to be a good observer, and why, by being a good observer, one can produce records.

What is the link between records and observation? The record must be a particular kind of speech. It must not exist merely as itself (as speech). It must exist as a reflection of its topic, i.e., as a reflection of events. The question is: how can one go about producing this kind of speech? We shall note that one can produce such speech by being an observer. In the literature, the question of what an observer is (and how, if at all, he can be said to be speaking) is, like the question of what a record is, not really answered. Selltiz's description of observation can serve as an example:[2]

> We are all constantly observing – noticing what is going on
> around us. We look out the window in the morning to see
> whether the sun is shining or whether it is raining, and
> make our decision about carrying an umbrella accordingly. If
> we are driving, we look to see whether the traffic light is red
> or green. . . . There is no need to multiply examples; as long
> as we are awake, we are almost constantly engaged in
> observation. It is our basic method of getting information
> about the world around us.

We agree with Selltiz that multiplying examples will not help,
but have the examples which she does give really helped
either? Is not her problem that all she can do is give examples?
That this quotation does not permit us to understand what is
distinctive to the activity of observation can be seen if we try to
consider the proffered 'definition'. We are supposedly observing when we notice. Would Selltiz want to say, then, that
everything we notice is an observation? If we notice that Selltiz
has produced an inadequate definition, is that an observation?
Perhaps it is, but then should we not wonder why Selltiz did
not notice that herself? Do some of us, then, observe (notice?)
better than others? If so, is it only the good observer who
notices or are we to say instead that we all notice different
things? If we take this tack, what are we to do with the Selltiz
notion that what we notice is what is going on around us? Are
different things going on around all of us and do their differences depend on us? Maybe Selltiz would want to distinguish
what is going on from what we only think is going on. Would
she say that thinking is not noticing? What is the difference
between noticing and thinking you notice? Moving on to the
window example, Selltiz seems to want to distinguish looking
and seeing. What is this distinction getting at? Sometimes, it
seems, we can look without seeing. Does noticing involve both
of these activities or only one? Are there other ways of seeing
besides looking? If there are, should we classify these as observation? With regard to Selltiz's version of what we see when
we look, 'what is going on' and, later, 'the world around us'
are singularly uninformative phrases. Exactly *what* is going on
around observers? One thing? Many things? What kinds of
things?

We ask all of these questions, not to immediately answer them, but to suggest the need for a fresh investigation of what the action of adequate observation might amount to. Our suggestion is that it amounts to producing the kind of speech exemplified in the idea of a record. Does this mean that Selltiz is wrong to identify observing with noticing? Is observing a kind of speaking rather than a kind of noticing? Or is the noticing Selltiz refers to perhaps her (vague) way of referring to the kind of speech observers are supposed to make. Maybe observers say something by putting into words what they have noticed. On the other hand, one can presumably say something without having noticed anything. We are back to the idea that records are, and observers make, a particular kind of speech. Do they make such speech by noticing what is going on? If so, we shall have to try to describe what it is to notice and what it is that is 'going on'.

1

At the heart of all of these issues is the question of what an observer is. Let us begin with a discussion of what is meant by the activity of observing. To be an observer is to be present, to 'be there'. Being there can be conceived, albeit vaguely, as being in the presence of whatever one is claiming to observe. If one is not present, if one is not 'there' in the present, then whatever one is doing one is not observing. However, although the observer must be concretely present, he is not supposed to make a difference. The contact of observation must be direct and unidirectional in that the contact flows from event to observer, so that the record can be direct and unencumbered by the observer's opinion. The observer must be disciplined and watch over any impulse to participate and thus contaminate the unidirectional flow. The reader of any record can believe he is reading a record if he can also believe the record is a reproduction of such unidirectional contact.

Observing can be distinguished from activities as diverse as theorizing, reminiscing, and expecting. For one thing, the latter do not require one to be present with the object of one's theorizing, reminiscing, or expecting. For another, these activities may actually thwart observation:[3]

> Expectation or anticipation frequently leads a witness astray. Those who count on revolutionaries to be bloodthirsty and conservatives to be gentlemen . . . usually find bloodthirsty revolutionaries and gentlemanly conservatives.

It is perhaps obvious that Gottschalk fails to come to grips with his own version of observation here. Suppose, as Gottschalk recommends, one does not anticipate. Does one then not find bloodthirsty revolutionaries and how is this not itself a result of lack of anticipation? How is the negative of anticipation different in principle from anticipating and then finding what one has anticipated? Apparently what Gottschalk thinks is important is that the observer should *not* do something, in this case expect or anticipate. By not doing these things one is somehow able to avoid being led astray. The observer, although he must be present, is being asked to negate himself in some interesting but unspecified ways. He is not to expect or anticipate and somehow what he does not do is going to make him into an adequate witness. Is there a positive version of what the observer should do available to someone, if not to Gottschalk, or is Gottschalk's emphasis on what observers should *not* do perhaps his (vague) way of saying that the action of observation is essentially negative, the action of observation requires not having an effect. Observers must be there and yet they are not supposed to make their presence felt.

Methodologists concerned with the problem of observation generally presuppose the simple fact that observing requires presence, and ignore the idea that while the observer must be present, so must he be absent in so far as he is not to participate in that with which he is to be present. The issue surfaces in the literature on participant observation and the argument of whether it should be overt or covert. That it should be covert suggests that the observer gets in the way of the record by having joined as a co-speaker what would otherwise be a univocal event. That it may have to be overt suggests that observation nevertheless must be a certain kind of presence, namely a presence which organizes itself to be in a position when the event reveals itself. Finally, that he must at least be covertly present and not away at his home reaffirms that presence is essential. Dalton, for example, never questions this requirement but stresses possible effects:[4]

[The observer's] presence may disturb the very situation he is seeking to freeze for study. . . .

Weick:[5]

> Observers are perceptable as well as perceptive. They are usually present in any observational situation. Whether this presence alters the course of a natural event is the concern of every person who uses observational methodology.

Note that we are given the same peculiar concern here. On the one hand, we are to be physically present; on the other, we are not to make a difference. We are to be present in the one sense, yet absent in the other.

The link between presence and the ability to observe can be seen in the plotting which novelists must go through in order to put their narrators at the scene of an incident. Hawthorne, for example, puts Roger Coverdale, the narrator of *The Blithedale Romance*, at a hotel window, in a treehouse, and behind a tombstone in order that he can be present at scenes about which Hawthorne wants his reader informed.[6] In moving Coverdale into strange locations, Hawthorne is relying on the two ideas that narrators cannot observe unless they are present but also cannot be effective observers if their presence imposes itself on the events.

Such machinations in order to maintain a presence which will not make a difference are not limited to first person narrators. It is a commonplace that social scientists engage in similar procedures:[7]

> In attempts to disguise the fact that observation is taking place, observers have hidden under beds in college dormitories, eavesdropped on conversations in theatre lobbies and along streets and posed as radio interviewers.

Most medical records depend for their adequacy on the implicit claim of the record-writer to have 'been there'. If we could imagine some reader challenging the following nurse's note by asking how the nurse knows these facts, the emphatic answer would be that she knows these facts because she observed them – because she was 'there'.

> 12:30 a.m. patient has no special rate, no respiration noted.

25

> Dr Jones notified and responded immediately. Patient
> pronounced expired 12:45 a.m. Family visits. No consent for
> post mortem obtained.

Noting the exact time of events, a common technique in medical records, whatever other functions it may have, certainly
serves to support the implicit claim that the nurse was 'there'.
At the same time, the nurse's having been there is not to be
seen as the point of the record. If we read this note as a record,
it is not the fact of the nurse's speech, not the existence of the
nurse, to which we are meant to attend. The speech and the
nurse are mere vehicles for the transmission of the real object
of interest: things she speaks 'about'. The record is the event to
the extent that we see the nurse's speech as not making any
difference. The nurse *qua* speaker should cease to matter since
her speech is supposed to amount to nothing but a representation of other things (the patient's death, the doctor's response,
the post mortem, etc.). The thingness of her speech and the
thereness of the nurse cease to matter if she succeeds in denying the fact of her speech by making her speech totally dependent on something other than itself, in this case, the events.

In the following psychiatric record, both the use of quotations and the reference to the author's (nurse's) involvement in
the events help to establish the writer's presence at the
reported events:

> [The patient] approached Mr Wagner and asked if he
> wanted to be 'smacked on the behind. One shot will get you
> out. Why marry and ruin some girl's life, anyway?' Reluctant
> to talk when nurse [the record-writer] tried to engage him in
> conversation on his feelings.

Although the record-writer does, in a sense, enter this record,
she enters it not through her speech but as another object
which her speech can disclose. The writer becomes 'the nurse',
merely another thing to be spoken about rather than the participant who made the speech. Again speech has been subju-
gated by being made the servant of its subject, the subject in
this case happening to include the record-writer.

This example helps to clarify how what sociologists refer to
as participant observation does not necessarily threaten the

basic idea of observation. The observer can participate as long as he is able to treat his participation as merely another thing to be spoken about. Like the nurse, then, the participant observer makes himself into one of his topics but also like the nurse he still succeeds in observing if he can treat his speech not as a fact in its own right but as dependent on what it is about, i.e., its subject, which in this case happens to include himself. More obviously, although both nurse and participant observer can participate in the sense that they can be part of the scene which they describe, neither is supposed to impose himself on the event. Usually their participation is limited to 'drawing out' what is thought to be there already. Thus in the record just quoted we are to focus on the patient's reluctance. That is the 'fact' the record brings to us rather than, for example, the fact that the nurse talked to the patient. Again we have the nurse's presence not as making a difference but merely as prod to help bring out what is really there, in this case the patient's reluctance.

Just as record-writers can claim to know the facts because they were present when they occurred, they can claim *not* to know the facts because they were physically absent. There are, of course, parts of the medical record which describe events which have occurred when the record-writer was *not* there. For example, all charts must include a 'history' of the events leading up to the illness for which the patient has been hospitalized. Obviously, doctors who take histories have not been present at these events. When items of this sort are included in the record, record-writers will be careful to note that what is reported is mere hearsay. They cannot certify the accuracy of the information in the record precisely because they were not 'present' when the events happened. A description of a patient's 'complaint' reads, 'Patient states that she took overdose of Seconal', reminding the reader that only the patient's version of what happened is being reported. In this case, the writer is clearly denying that *she* can know what happened, because she was not there.[8] More precisely, when recording 'hearsay', record-writers are continuing to follow observers' principles. The difference between 'hearsay' and other events is that in 'hearsay' what the record-writer can know (as observer) is not what happened but what the patient *says* has happened. The event with which the record-writer is present is the patient's speech. This speech is treated in the same way any other event is treated, that is, it is treated as a thing to be disclosed by treating one's own speech as mere vehicle for the disclosure of what the record is really 'about', in this case the patient's speech. Although hearsay is usually formulated as information at second remove, really it is (as the word implies) information at first hand, but about what someone has said. Of course, given an interest in the 'original' event, the problem represented by hearsay is that there have been twice as many chances for the observer's rule to be violated, twice as many chances for speakers to fail to control their speech so as to let the event speak through them.

Since records are written by observers and observing depends upon presence, record-writers leave gaps for the periods when they cannot be with patients:

> Patient out on day-pass, due to return 11:00 p.m. Didn't.

> 4:00 p.m. has not returned. 7:00 p.m. still not back from pass.

> Patient went to the operating room and returns back to the floor.

These writers are not being good *reporters* in that they are leaving out crucial (yet according to the observer, only opinionated and not knowledgeable) information such as what happened while the patients were away from the hospital or in the operating room. They are, however, being good *observers* by showing their ignorance about events from which they are absent.

The connection of observing to presence suggests a very simple, albeit partial, explanation for the abundance of records in complex organizations in modern society.[9] It may not be sufficient to our understanding of records to say that organizations require rational, efficient, and objective observations and therefore require employees to be present in order to make the observations.[10] Perhaps organizations require employees to produce observations in order to motivate employees to be present at events they would otherwise avoid. Thus, there are two ways to account for the fact that all hospital nurses must write one record every day for every patient. The hospital needs daily records, but also the fact that they must write a daily record forces nurses to see patients they might otherwise miss.

2

We shall return here to the observer's dilemma with regard to his concurrent presence and absence if he is to be able to record. The observer is to be there but he is not to participate. He is to speak but not to make the fact of his speech the point of his speech. What are we to make of this peculiar and on the face of it contradictory set of actions and omissions? A record is made by one who is present in time (the observer). Somehow the observer's presence enables the record and, through the connection noted in chapter 1, the event as well, to last or become eternal. The event becomes known in so far as there is a record of it. How is the presence of a record made to equal the presence of knowledge? If the event appears to a present observer, it can become knowledge if the observer can deny that the record is an achievement of his participation in the event. That is, an observer needs to be present but is not supposed to have participated in the creation of the event if the record is to be treated as knowledge. Recorders, then, are observers of spectacle; they are present but do not participate. In this sense they are an absent presence. The achievement of the observer is the achievement of absence through presence. The responsible observer is one who can make what he observes responsible for what he records.

What is eternal about records, as in the notion of an archive, is achieved by the process of divorcing the record from its maker. If the record is devoid of any contamination arising from the observer's participation, then record users can know the event through the record because, since the record has not been affected by the observer, it becomes unnecessary to understand the observer in order to understand the record. The record speaks for itself. If an observer is present then he can know about a present event. That the observer is no longer present and that the event is a thing of the past can be irrelevant since, through the record, the observer has become irrelevant.

To observe, then, is to be a spectator. To be a spectator is to show the capacity to record. The spectator, if he can be said to participate at all, participates not as co-speaker with the event, but as passive observer of the thing which is the event, identical with the things which are the words of the report. Through the segregation of the observer from the record, the record is made to stand by itself. Analytically speaking, the observer might as well not be there, and we have formulated how he is not there. In this analytic regard there is no essential difference between the observer who presents himself as such and the one who observes in secret, since the achievement of the admitted observer is that he is not there at all, whatever the actual circumstances in which he makes the record. Kaplan has remarked that 'observation means that special care is being taken: the root meaning of the word is not just to "see", but to watch over.'[11] We are arguing that the observer must take special care to avoid intruding on and hence affecting the event. 'Watching over', then, is not to watch *over* the event in the sense that one must control its production, but merely to watch it given the negation of participation by the self. What is 'watched over' is the self, so that the self can be said to be indifferent to the watched event in order that appearances can show themselves as events. What 'makes the record' is the event and not the observer. Making a record is at most noting the appearance. In this way the most important activity of the observer is not to make the record but to make ready so that the event can make the record – to be ready so that the event can present itself. The observer makes ready by segregating his speech (the record) from himself (that he makes the record).

Presence, then, should be used by the observer as a method for permitting the indifferent recording of spectacle. The observer's indifference – the fact that he does not make a difference to the event – is what makes the event eternal, always present, and not subject to further transformation. The observer can adequately record the appearance of things by watching over any impulse to join them. What he watches over is the continued segregation of speech from speaker which simultaneously neutralizes the speech and socializes the event.

The permanent presence of the event through its record is achieved by the obliteration of that which could make a difference to the event. What could make a difference is a co-speaker. The co-speaker is obliterated by having the event speak alone through the record. The absence of a participant factualizes the event as a record and thus makes the event eternal. The event is permanently present if, through the denial of the effects of his participation, the recorder has managed to make a record which amounts to nothing but the original event. The observer makes a record by making himself into nothing. As the observer becomes irrelevant, the event becomes permanently present.

There is an irony overriding our formulation which now can be made explicit. The observer desires the permanent presence of the human event or human history through the survival of the record. Yet in order to ensure such survival the observer seems to sacrifice his own humanity or life in that he leads the deadly life of indifference. The survival of the event seems to require lifelessness from the observer. That observing results in the pain of lifelessness gives an incentive to an inquiry into how observers come to choose such a painful life.

Presence might be formulated as life and absence as death so permanent presence amounts to eternal life. Like most men, the observer fears death. He deals with the fear by seeking to ensure that he lives, i.e., survives and that even after death he will be preserved in the form of his remains. In keeping records the observer does for others exactly what his commitment to presence indicates that he wants others to do for him, i.e., ensure survival.

Even though ensuring survival may seem the most natural and reasonable thing to do, right off it resonates with greed. Greed has a very strong sense of desire, in the case of gluttony for food, in the case of capitalism for money. Seeking permanent presence amounts to greed for life: it simply wants as much of it as possible. If we can understand the trouble with greed, perhaps we can also understand the trouble with permanent presence. Greed, like permanent presence, has as a necessary feature the desire to be unending. The glutton never wants to stop eating; the capitalist wants more and more money; the observer wants the event to survive for ever. What

31

the greedy lack, then, is a sense of the good of an end. The glutton argues that since food is good why not keep eating for ever, the observer that since life is good why not live for ever. But such reasoning misunderstands desire. Food is one thing we sometimes desire. The good of food is that it ends our hunger. Understanding our desire for food requires that we have a sense of how to end the desire. The point is not to sustain our desire to eat but to find the way to fulfil it. The end of the desire need not be a problem since it can be thought of as fulfilment. Fulfilling desires requires understanding what will end them. The very idea of desire, then, makes reference to the good of ends or limits as that which fulfils and in that sense ends the desire.

The glutton's mistake is to confuse the desire itself with its end. If desire itself is made the end, the desire will have no end and so will be unending. Greed is unfulfilling in that it is the permanent presence of a desire without the corresponding and necessary sense of the reason, and therefore potential end, of the desire. Hence the capitalist mindlessly accumulating and the glutton eating more and more and never satisfied.

The problem, then, is not that the observer desires life but that the observer thinks that it is enough to have this desire without fulfilling it. Converting the desire for life into an end means that instead of trying to think of how to fulfil the desire, instead of pursuing a good end, the observer thinks only about how to sustain the desire, i.e., make life unending. Any end – death, revolution, causes, the desire to be heard or participate – appears not as something to be thought about which might fulfil the life but only as an external threat or danger. Death loses its primordial place as the natural end of life and becomes one such threat to be avoided at all costs. The greedy life becomes not a life of desire but a life of fear, fear of death, fear of any difference at all, since difference forcibly reminds the observer that there is other than his desire and so his desire may end. Thought itself becomes not a way of fulfilling desire but a threat to desire in that it deliberates about ends and does not just sustain beginnings.

3

Thus far we have described observing as an activity which achieves absence through presence as its way of obtaining knowledge. Let us now attempt to establish the possibility of this accepted link between observing and knowledge. Our question is: how must knowledge be conceived in order that the idea of presence could be a means of obtaining that knowledge? We must attempt to formulate the conception of knowledge which makes the idea of an observer possible and necessary as a means to obtain that knowledge.

The observer can be described as solving the problem of knowledge by being there, by presence. The solution embodied in the observer is just one possible solution to the problem of knowledge, however. It is a solution which makes observing (presence) reasonable, but it is only a solution to a particular and differentiated version of the problem of knowledge.

Our question now is: for what version of the problem of knowledge could presence, could the observer's kind of being there, be a solution? To answer this question is to characterize the particular conception of the problem of knowledge which is presupposed in the idea of observing. When the problem of knowledge is constrained by a certain conception of time and place, then the idea of an observer, of presence, could be a solution to the problem of knowledge. Our task is to explicate the conception of time and place which makes an observer necessary.

Time[12]

By thinking of himself historically (as a being in time) man makes the relationship between self and knowledge into a contingency. Man is not knowledge (since he is finite). Man is he who can do the knowing. The distinction between self and knowledge makes man's ability to know into only a possibility, thus laying the basis for a distinction between knowledge (what is known) and opinion (what man only thinks he knows). We shall be concerned only with one particular way of differentiating knowledge and opinion. The form of the distinction with which we are concerned is achieved by detaching the self from the world and treating the self's speech as only problematically connected to the world which that speech is 'about'. The contingency of knowledge resides here in various possible relations between speaker and world. The practical question of knowing becomes: how to assure the kind of relation that would produce knowledge rather than opinion? Given the problematic status of the relationship between speech and world, one answer to the problem is to treat speech as true speech only if speech and world are 'together', i.e., only if the speech can be segregated from the man (the speaker) and given to the world. By transfer, as it were, the world is made to speak for itself, because it is made devoid of participation by the man who would raise anew the very problem of knowledge which this particular relation is meant to solve. In effect, the observer is generated by making him speechless, a witness to a world which testifies for itself.

What is known is thus what is witnessed as the world's speech. What is known is the witness's transcription of the world's speech. What is known is limited to the circumscribed and local coalescence of the event and observer. With regard to time, local coalescence is achieved through co-presence of world and witness. Time is itself conceived to both enable and inhibit a relation of local co-presence which determines that which can be known and that which cannot. The future cannot be known and the past cannot be known but the present can be, and thus the problem of knowledge is reasserted as the twin barriers of past and future. Given the problem of knowledge, an observer constituted by presence solves the problem in this domain by, again, localizing the relation between self and world (here, that part of the world that passes by). The fact of his presence shows that he recognizes his version of the problem of knowledge, i.e., his presence suggests that he recognizes that neither the future nor the past can be known but the present can.

Riley states that:[13]

> The method [observation] is applicable to action taking place only in the present. It obviously cannot be used to refer to periods prior to the inception of the research.

However, to state that observing is 'inapplicable' to past and future fails to preserve the action of observers as they achieve their relation to the present. It is not that observing is 'inapplicable' to the past and future but that the idea of observing (presence) expresses the basic conception that neither the past nor the future can be known and only the present can be. An observer's whole reason for existence depends upon the idea that only the present can be known.

If observing is grounded in the idea that only the present can be known, record-writers, *in so far as they are acting as observers*, should express ignorance about both the past and the future. Thus writers who refer to the future tend to be uncertain about it as if what they write is only an opinion and thus defeasible:

He is to be discharged in a.m. if all goes well.

If he remains relatively calm through the weekend we will be home free.

Waiting for results of lung scan.

Even when the future is a *medical* certainty, record-writers *qua* observers will express doubt. Even when their 'medical' opinion is that patients will certainly die, record-writers will write:

Patient looks moribund and is bleeding uncontrollably from two puncture sites.

Prognosis extremely poor.

Condition is very poor.

In so far as they are acting as observers, medical record-writers will also be uncertain about the past:

Had *possible* seizure after which was found in bed with burning mattress. *Question of* smoking in bed [My emphasis].

The nurse can be certain about the event she observes (the burning mattress), but she can only guess about what may have occurred earlier (a seizure, smoking in bed).[14]

It must be stressed that we are grounding [15] the role of observer and not making factual statements about the past, the

35

present, the future. We shall soon suggest how Socrates is unwilling to be restricted by the exigency that is time. Even from some conventional viewpoints, of course, access to the past is held to be possible, hence history, archaeology, and geology. Similarly, to rule out talk of the future would eliminate both the scientific activity of predicting and the common-sense activity of expecting. It is also no fact that the present *can* be known, since, about many current events, we will be clearer tomorrow than we are today. We are not suggesting how past, present, and future must universally be seen; we are suggesting how *observers* must see the past, the present, and the future for their activity, i.e., presence, to make sense. Ours is a formulation of a formulation necessary to make the activity of observation intelligible. Thus, we are not saying that the past cannot be known. We are saying that in so far as one believes that the past can be known one thereby eliminates the necessity for observing that past when it was present.

When a historian can write that: 'the intellectual fascination which underlies the form of history is the desire to understand the meaning of what has happened in former times',[16] he is defining himself as other than an observer precisely by treating the past as knowable *without* his having been there. In so far as archaeologists, geologists, or psychiatrists can treat the present as permitting inferences about the past, they can make it unnecessary that they be present in the past in order to know it, i.e., they can make it unnecessary that they be observers of that past when it was present.

Similarly, in so far as one can claim to know the future, whether by prediction, prophecy, or expectation, one eliminates the need to observe that future when it becomes present; one is eliminating the need to 'wait and see'. Waiting and seeing, i.e., observing, is only necessary when the future can be treated as unknowable.[17]

Finally, the notion that the present can be known is not a general principle; it is an observer's principle. If one treats the present as unknowable as, for example, sceptical philosophers do, one can thereby make it seem unreasonable to observe the present.[18]

Place

Just as observing is grounded in a particular conception of time, it is also grounded in a particular conception of place. The observer's rule for overcoming place as a barrier to know-ledge is again to transfer responsibility for the speech to the world by making the relationship between the speech and the world into a local relation: only places at which one is present can be known.[19] One can know a place, as an observer, only by being there. Just as observers can know only the present, so can they know only places at which they have been present.

Again it should be stressed that to conceive of place as a barrier to knowledge which can be overcome by presence is not the only possible conception of place. Jaded travellers and other cynics think all places are basically the same and that, therefore, it is unnecessary to go to the place to know it. Physi-cists can formulate laws which are independent of place and social scientists can posit cultural universals. Common-sense actors do not always assume that they do not know a place because they have not been there. Thus even 'newcomers' can have expectations.

The point is not some factual assertion that only places to which one has gone can be known. The point is that in so far as one is committed to the activity of observing, one can only achieve an observation through the grammar of suspended judgment about places at which one has not been.[20]

In ordinary usage, we consider the two meanings of 'pres-ent' with which we have been concerned to be distinct. We distinguish being here in time (the present) and being here in space (presence). However, the observer inhabits both spheres at once, being present in time and in space in order to extract the world's testimony through witness. The concept of pres-ence is meant to capture the fact that observers stand in the same relation to time and to place as a way of achieving the local relation of coalescence which enables them to know. Pre-sence is identical with the world-as-speaker, with knowledge. The observer's reason for being present in time is the same as his reason for being present in space, namely to subjugate his speech, which would only be opinion, to the discipline of par-ticipant self-denial. Whatever is foreign about space and time –

however they are barriers to knowledge – is concealed from himself by the observer in his refusal to speak of them.

Since the observer is *refusing* to speak of what he does not know, we can say that his silence is not inevitable. Socrates says he does not know anything and yet he certainly does not refuse to speak. For example, in the *Phaedo* he is willing to speak about the future rewards of a good life while admitting that he does not know if what he says is correct. He refers to his speech as a 'noble risk'. All speech for Socrates is trying to formulate the good, and therefore all speech amounts to a noble risk in that it is worth risking being wrong if even when one happens to be wrong one is attempting to formulate and hence do good. Socrates knows that he does not know, i.e., he knows that the best he can do is intend to do good, whereas the observer seeks relief from this noble uncertainty.

The observer sees rightly that Socrates is taking risks with his speech, e.g., by talking of past and future, but fails to see that the risks are worth taking. He comes to see Socrates as merely irresponsible, as indulging in the luxury of opinions while foolishly ignoring the danger of being wrong. The observer's response is to deprive himself of the opinions in order to minimize the risk of failing (being wrong). His version of knowledge as witnessing appears to him as a responsible abnegation of the temptation of opinions. We have already discussed various instances of this self-deprivation, e.g., the observer's commitment to assertion over explication, copying over originating, being ruled over reasoning. He seems safe from the risk of being wrong because to be wrong one has to express an opinion and the observer refuses to express his. Socrates' point to him is that his safety is only apparent because his attempts to minimize the risk of being wrong have unintentionally exposed him to the greater danger of doing himself harm. The observer has forgotten that he needs to decide whether a given action is good for him in order to decide whether it is truly safe for him. Deciding whether an action is good must involve talking of its future, e.g., of its intended outcome, its possible rewards. The observer's desire never to be wrong (never to have to speak of the future) becomes a refusal to discuss the good of any action. This refusal will lead the responsible observer (the observer who wants to do good) to a desire never to have to act. Inaction amounts to the attempt to be indifferent to the difference between what he thinks would be good for him and what he thinks would be bad for him and so the observer will inevitably let the bad happen to him without doing anything about it. He lets what he *thinks* is bad happen to him because he does not *know* it is bad. Instead of possibly doing good (taking the noble risk), the observer is definitely not doing good even though he wants to.

In terms of the current metaphor, we *are* asking the observer to speak of the future. Yet, contrary to how the observer hears the request, we are not asking for irresponsible speech. The future is the sense of the good which makes purposeful whatever one is doing in the present so what we want the observer to say is why he thinks silence (about past, future, and for that matter present) is better than speech. Implicit in our desire for the observer to speak is the point that the observer cannot avoid doing what he thinks is good, if only be silent, and so for his own good should take responsibility for his opinions. Once the observer can see that he has an opinion rather than knowledge, once he sees that the issue is always what he thinks is good, he will be able to see that it was he rather than Socrates who was irresponsible. While Socrates would observe only when he thinks it was better to observe, the observer was actually observing even in spite of his best judgment in the vain hope of avoiding judgments (responsibility).

4

In this chapter, our task is to address the grounds for seeing records as facts or truth. Although observing has been discussed more directly than recording, in an important sense the task of grounding records has already been at least partially accomplished.[21] For we shall next show how an analysis of observing is also an analysis of recording, since the activity of observing entails the activity of recording. We shall discuss two questions: (1) Why an observer can make a record. (2) Why records are necessary at all. Neither question is adequately discussed in the literature. Selltiz furnishes an example of how the record-observer link is usually formulated. Selltiz states that 'in recording unstructured observation, two questions require consideration: When should the observer make notes? How should notes be kept?'[22] To ask these questions is to treat our questions as already answered. That an observer should take notes presupposes, of course, that an observer *can* take notes. Observers *can* take notes only because they can do the kind of action we have explicated in this chapter. That is, essential to the activity of taking notes in Selltiz's sense is the activity of taking note in an observer's sense. Observers can take the kind of notes we presume Selltiz would want them to take only in so far as they can *take note*. Taking note is another word for the action of observation: treating one's speech not as a fact in its own right, not as participation, but as a product of events. Notes, then, are nothing but a written down version of the action engaged in by the competent observer. Observation amounts to taking note not because concrete observers take notes but because being an observer amounts to making a particular kind of speech. In being an observer one is not, as we have said, participating through one's speech. The speech one makes through observing amounts to listening, to hearing from things what to say about them. Thus, the speech an observer makes amounts to taking note – not contributing to things but merely attending to what is already there. Our analysis of observation is also an analysis of recording in the sense that a record is nothing but an observer's version of speech – speech which does not make a difference but merely notes whatever is there to be seen.

In the following quotation, we can see how Selltiz conceals the analytic identity between observation and the kind of speech observers make (taking note):[23]

> The best time for recording is undoubtedly on the spot and during the event. This results in a minimum of selective bias and distortion through memory. There are many situations, however, in which note-taking on the spot is not feasible, because it would disturb the naturalness of the situation or arouse the suspicions of the persons observed. . . . Constant note-taking may interfere with the quality of observation. The observer may easily lose relevant aspects of the situation if he divides his attention between observing and writing.

To say that there are 'many situations in which note-taking on the spot is not feasible' is to obscure the fact that to observe *is* to take note. The observer may not write it down on the spot, but that he does not is not to say that he has not taken note in the sense of listened to what the event has to say. Indeed, he can only 'decide' between writing it down now and later because, having assimilated the event through observation, what he would say later can be the same as what he would say now since in both cases it is the permanent, unchanging event which his speech is supposed to reveal. Selltiz worries that the observer's memory may fail him, but this worry covers over the more basic point that the observer has some thing to remember. He has some thing to remember only because he has succeeded in making ready so that a thing could reveal itself to him. That 'constant note-taking may interfere with observation' and that the observer may 'divide his attention between observing and writing' make it sound as if observing and writing are two different activities. Concretely they are, of course, but, analytically, what the observer writes is circumscribed by what he has observed. What he should write has been determined for him by what has happened. Basically, what he should write has already been said since it is the event which tells him what to say about it.

The next question we want to raise is why observers must speak at all – why a record is necessary. Given the analysis just completed, to observe *is* to make the recorder's kind of speech. Our question now is *why* observing takes the form of taking note. We shall argue that observing, to make sense, must *always* result in some kind of a record. Whether the record takes the form of writings, tape recording, pictures, or memories is irrelevant at the present level of abstraction. Whereas methodologists emphasize the differences between written records and memories, the former supposedly doing the job better than the latter, we have already suggested how they both are different ways to do the same thing (take note) and now we shall suggest how they both have the same justification. The observer seems to produce a kind of product, a set of notes or his 'memories', and it is these that constitute the knowledge he has obtained. In most discussions about observation it is simply assumed that observing requires recording.

Selltiz, as quoted above, by focusing on when and how to take notes, certainly does not ask why notes are necessary in the first place. Similarly, although Cicourel notes that 'the group's activities may not permit recording of events until a considerable time between observation and recording has elapsed',[24] he does not investigate why observers record. We shall ask what there is about observing such that recording (or remembering) is necessary.

The usual answer to this question will not be acceptable to us. The usual answer is that observers must take notes or keep records because their memories are fallible. As Simon puts this position:[25]

[Observing] . . . requires immediate and detailed reporting whenever possible. Anthropologists try to record their field notes every day, to minimize the chance that their memories will play tricks on them. Police officers are also trained to take on-the-spot notes, to prevent bias and inaccuracy from creeping in. . . .

The commonplace view that records are necessary because observers, being human, tend to forget, begs our question. It is only noteworthy that observers tend to forget because observers are supposed to remember. It is the need for remembering which makes the observer's forgetfulness into a problem and also makes notes necessary as a way of overcoming the problem. Therefore, the burden of our analysis will be to show why observers must remember as a way of depicting why a record (or a memory) is necessary for one to claim he has adequately observed. Simon's attempt to explain the need for records is based on a physical fact.[26] He thinks he can explain the need for records by citing an obvious fact about memories, i.e., that they 'play tricks'. However, while the physical fact may tell us why memories fail, it does not tell us why memories are necessary in the first place. We shall suggest that it is not physical facts but the grounds of the activity of observing, as they have already been formulated, which make remembering necessary and, therefore, make necessary devices for remembering such as records and memories.

Why does observing always require some kind of a record? It has already been suggested that to observe is to be able to know the present but not the past or future. Now it must be noted that there is an obvious defect in the knowledge of the observer, as he has been defined to this point. The observer can know only the present. The defect in the knowledge of the observer so defined has to do with the obvious fact that the present becomes the past. Because the present becomes the past, the observer stands to lose every last bit of knowledge that he ever gained, since, when the present becomes the past, he should, *qua* observer, cease to know it.

Given that observing requires presence, it is possible that the observer's knowledge will become ephemeral, that he will never be able to accumulate knowledge. It must be stressed that the fact that observers can lose all of their knowledge is not a physiological given but a consequence of the socially organized identity of observing itself. Forgetting becomes possible because of the various stipulations concerning the problem of knowledge and its solution, as mentioned above, which create the possibility of observation as an intelligible activity: first, time is passing (the present is becoming the past), and second, observers can know only the present. Thus, unless observing is to result in only the most transient kind of knowledge, some device is required for freezing the observed present before it becomes the foreign past. It is as a service to the longevity of the present that records fit into our analysis. The record overcomes the pastness of what was once present by converting the present into the permanent. Records are made necessary by the basic idea that only the present can be known.

Many writers have stated that records are characterized by *permanence*. For example, Wheeler writes: '[records] have a permanence lacking in informal communication.'[27] Weick writes: 'If an observer obtains a record of a natural event . . . he . . . has a permanent picture of what occurred.'[28] We are noting more than the permanence of records, however. We are now in a position to understand *why* observers want a 'permanent picture': to record is to make the present into the permanent, to make the present remain, and making the present remain becomes necessary when one believes, as observers do, that when the present becomes the past it can no longer be known.

The record thus makes the present permanent and eternalizes the event. The event speaks for ever through the record, the record being identical with the event. Just as the problematic relation of knower to known is overcome by the witnessed but univocal speech of the event, so do we continue to subdue any co-participation, and therefore any doubt, by externalizing this selfsame event in the transcription which is the record.[29] That we are not to co-participate with the event in making the record is of course a nearly perfect example of depersonalization. We can see, however, that the kind of depersonalization represented by the record, i.e., the idea that the observer should render himself speechless, is not bureaucratic miscarriage, but bureaucratic necessity according to this very bureaucratic version of knowledge. Analytically speaking, the recorded past is the present so depersonalization is necessary if the very claim to know anything but the present moment is to be possible.[30]

We have described an observer's kind of speech (taking note) and we have tried to show why he must make this kind of speech. However, it should be clear that the kind of speech an observer is supposed to make is very different from the opinions his whole activity is supposed to overcome. The observer's speech (record) does not make a difference to the event. It does not change it. Rather, it eternalizes it. The observer, through his speech, has not produced the event, he has preserved it. If his speech does finally make a difference to the event it is not so much what his speech does *to* the event. It is what his speech does *for* the event. Unlike the event, the speech lasts but what lasts as long as the speech lasts is not (in any important sense) the speech but the event the speech is serving.

This idea of records provides a more complete formulation of the observer's relation to past and future.[31] It is not enough to say that the observer cannot know the past. He cannot know it *qua* past, certainly, but he can know it in the form of the 'formerly present' (and, for the future, the 'will be present').[32]

We are offering here a special formulation of the very mundane fact that observers can know the past if they were present when it was the present.[33] One can remember for the record. Just as it is not enough to say the observer cannot know the past, neither is it enough to say the record is only something material like a past sentence or photograph done simultaneously with the event. The event speaks through the observer, and so any speech, so long as it can be determined that the speech is the event's speech, can make a record. Given the grounds discussed above, those committed to observation would not ask whether a memory could be a record any more than they would ask whether observation could be knowledge. Rather, the question of memory is technical and specific to particular instances: is this memory contaminated by participation extraneous to the event's own speech (forgetfulness, desire, the intrusion of exterior events, etc.)? Thus, record-writers can write about the past as long as they were present when it was the present, because we can continue to assume that it is the event which is speaking:

> I first saw the patient in November, 1967, for heartburn and constipation.

> Wife visited in a.m. Made comfortable.

> Ambulated length of hall with assistance.

> Refused a.m. care. Seen by Dr Saver.

Although the writers of these notes know the past, they do not know it *qua* past. They can know the past because they knew it when it was the present and by observing and recording it they convert it into the permanent.

Knowing the past *qua* past or, better, knowing that what came before has not really passed is Socrates' sense of remembering. The observer is frightened to forget for the understandable reason that he believes he is losing something if he forgets it. Socrates would remind him that forgetting is not permanently losing since we can remember as well as forget. The observer wants to insure against forgetfulness by remembering what he has not even forgotten yet. He thinks Socrates' admitted forgetfulness is too risky because it raises the possibility of not remembering. As usual there is more to Socrates' notion than meets the observer's eye. Socrates and Plato use our common experiences with remembering as a way of talking about our relationship to the good. Thus, although both Aristodemus and Apollodorus admit to having forgotten portions of the speeches at the Symposium, judging from the length of the speeches, they have managed to remember much more of what Socrates said than of what anyone else said. There is less danger of our forgetting the good than our forgetting the bad. More deeply, there is no danger in forgetting the bad because it is not worth remembering.

Part of the observer's fear of forgetting, then, is really his by now familiar unwillingness to differentiate good and bad. Since Plato, like the observer, does not *know* what is good it looks like he is taking an irresponsible risk in forgetting what he *thinks* is bad, e.g., in the case of the Symposium most of Phaedrus' speech and several entire speeches. The observer would have tried to save these because they could possibly be good. But Plato's real point is that the survival of Socrates' speech is not merely the fortunate event that historians believe the survival of any record is. Socrates does not have to ensure his survival at all in order to remain. Socrates is safe because what is best about him, i.e., his goodness, cannot perish. The observer seeks to remember everything for the understandable reason that he thinks the good will perish if he forgets it. On the other hand the Socratic dialogues show, not just with Aristodemus' and Apollodorus' good memories, but with the countless interchanges of Socrates and his interlocutors, that people can remember the good, e.g., the notion that no one does bad intentionally, the notion that friends will do one good, the notion that love is of the good, even if their actions indicate that they have forgotten the good. Since we can remember the good after having forgotten it, the observer's healthy fear of forgetting the good need not lead to his enterprise of trying to remember everything. Instead, he should seek to remember the good. Our analysis is actually suggesting that the observer has forgotten the good: he has forgotten what observing is good for, he has forgotten what the future is good for, he has forgotten what the past is good for. If he panics and thinks that he is therefore lost, he has also forgotten what remembering is for, namely to remind himself that while he has forgotten the good of his enterprise he has not therefore lost it. He can learn (recollect) what he is doing and therefore reachieve responsibility for his fate. By reachieving responsibility for his fate, he can learn again that the past has not passed, i.e., that he needs to learn from his mistakes and reproduce his successes since the selfsame opportunity to intend to do good will eternally arise.

3 Records and events

In chapter 2 it was emphasized that the observer-recorder's kind of presence becomes reasonable and even necessary only within a particular conception of time and place. When this viewpoint is developed, it has important practical implications: the simple fact that records must be produced by 'being there' predetermines certain characteristics of records and, even, of the world. We cannot accept the view that records are merely a passive and mechanical reproduction of 'what has happened'. If it can be said that the observer is passive, then we have tried to indicate in chapters 1 and 2 the very rigorous kind of *work* which is necessary to the achievement of this passivity. Nor can we accept the view that records are a biased representation of 'what has happened'. The bias of records – if it is anything – is surely not a description of what records are but a description of one thing that can happen to some (or all) of them, a happening which itself remains unexplicated and unprovided for until records are provided for. Both views are subject to the same criticism: they accept as given what records are 'about' – the world, events, what has happened – and then try to formulate how records stand in relation to that given. By contrast when records are seen in terms of the grounds which make them possible, it is no longer adequate to state that records reflect, whether accurately or inaccurately, the givens of the real world, because the real world itself comes to be shaped by the very idea of recording it.

When the grounds of recording are examined, the 'real' world ceases to be a given. Rather, the grounds which make it seem reasonable to write records determine in advance *both* the characteristics of actual records and of the 'real world' as it will appear to record-writers. *It is not that records record things but that the very idea of recording determines in advance how things will have to appear*. A record is a way of giving evidence, and a way of giving evidence is to record what one witnesses. Consequently, in so far as the 'real world' is constituted by and through its record, it is simultaneously constituted by and through the enforced conceptions of adequate evidence as witnessable evidence which create and limit the activity of observation.

In an argument which bears superficial similarity to this one, many authors have suggested that record-writers (and historians) must decide which facts are worth recording or interpreting. For example, Weick writes:[1]

> No recording system in current use provides an exact reproduction of an event, yet the fact that editing occurs is not always realized.

Schutz writes, concerning the historian's task:[2]

> The science of history has the momentous task of deciding which events, actions, and communicative acts to select for the interpretation and reconstruction of 'history' from the total social reality of the past.

E. H. Carr makes a similar point:[3]

> The historian is necessarily selective. The belief in a hard core of historical facts existing objectively and independently of the historian is a preposterous fallacy. . . .

According to these writers, the key problem which historians and observers face is 'selectivity'. Observers must decide which facts to 'select' from the myriad of 'actual' facts.

Since selectivity is essentially a notion which depends upon treating the real world as a given, i.e., as that from which the observer must select, the problem with the idea is that it does not go far enough. That from which this or that is selected remains unexamined and thus the selfsame world which provides for its extractability remains unexamined as well. For example, that selection is even possible requires among other things a version of the world as a witnessable world. The recorder, then, does not simply select. Rather, he relies on grounds. These grounds offer up the possibility of selection. Selection, then, cannot be formulated as simply a problem observers face, since the very fact that observers *can* select constitutes an affirmation that observers are confronting a world of potentially observable and recordable things. We shall show that it is not just that the observer must 'select' certain facts and leave out others. Rather, the grounds of the record-writer will force him to see *all* facts, both those he selects and those he omits as having a certain form since his grounds presuppose a particular concept of factuality. In other words, record-writers are not in a situation of looking at 'the' world and selecting parts of it. Rather, what their world consists of is determined by their grounds. It is these grounds which determine, for example, that the world *permits* a mining operation which does not contaminate the unextracted remainder left in the world. Mining or selecting does not make a difference; it leaves the world as it was. We note again the scaffold of observation as a support for non-participation, leaving the world observed yet unchanged by the fact that it has been observed and, furthermore, leaving the recorded event recorded yet unchanged by the fact that it has been recorded. In this sense the event is the record, the record the event. The observer is the recorder and the event is the record. The record is 'pure', i.e., its shape is identical with the shape of the event. Unless the world can be thought of as sets of events which can be extracted and yet not affected by the extraction process, the record can not equal the event. Thus, the very idea of seeing the world as divisible into events, the very notion of 'events', is made necessary by the grounds of the activity of recording.

Teggart, on the other hand, makes a clear distinction between records and events:[4]

> The historian concerns himself, on the one hand, with documents, and, on the other, with happenings or events which have taken place in the past. . . .

Similarly, Cicourel distinguishes 'natural occurrences' from information about them:[5]

> Our task is similar to that of constructing a computer that would reduce the information obtainable by means of the perspectives of differently situated video tapes, so that the information (or parts of it) could be retrieved while maintaining the fidelity of the original natural occurrence.

Teggart, Cicourel, and others[6] emphasize the distinction between records and events recorded as a technical matter and would seem to be attempting to reduce the technical disparity in such a way as to affirm the analytic equivalence between record and event. We shall investigate the *connection* between the idea of making a record and the idea of an event, a happening, an occurrence, the connection which produces their technical distinction. We shall attempt to show that the possibility that a record *could* represent the world or part of it and therefore the possibility that records could be grounded as we grounded them in chapter 2, depends on formulating the world as made up of witnessable events, of happenings, of occurrences to which observers can testify. From the viewpoint of the record-writer, it is not just that he must report accurately or even select from events in the world. Rather, the possibility and necessity of his writing a record at all depends on his seeing the world as a set of witnessable and extractable events.

The point that observing presupposes a particular conception of the world may seem bland unless we provide the alternative conception which is informing our work. Socrates speaks of himself as a midwife so he, too, might be said to be extracting events. Yet Socrates, unlike the observer, changes what he extracts in the sense that no speech event in the dialogues is left to stand as what it originally appears to be. We are back to the argument between Socrates and the observer with the observer now objecting that it is irresponsible of Socrates to change things since Socrates cannot know whether a change is for the better. But the changes that occur in the dialogues are not mere persuasion – Socrates is not telling people what to think; he is reminding people *to* think and such a reminder cannot be bad since no one will hurt himself intentionally (thinkingly). As just one example of why the observer should not fear Socrates, let us consider the exchange between Polemarchos, Socrates, and Glaucon which launches the *Republic*. As Socrates and Glaucon start back to Athens from Piraeus, Polemarchos and some friends stop them and Polemarchos seeks to keep Socrates in Piraeus by saying, 'Do you see how many we are? Are you stronger than all these? For, if not, you will have to remain where you are.' 'May there not be the alternative,' says Socrates, 'that we may persuade you to let us go?' 'But can you persuade us, if we refuse to listen to you?' 'Certainly not', says Glaucon.[7] The observer, unlike Polemarchos, will not use force. Nor can the observer see any good in persuasion because people do tend to refuse to listen and even if they do listen, he is not so sure of his own views that he would want to convince others of them. He therefore becomes Polemarchos' victim, forced because he is too principled to force and too modest to persuade. The observer would have had a boring time imprisoned in Piraeus, listening to Polemarchos, Thrasymachos, and the rest until they, probably bored as well, chose to let him return to Athens. Socrates takes the same situation and, with the help of the others, manages to generate the *Republic*.

The *Republic* is possible because, as Plato indicates by letting Glaucon answer Polemarchos' last question, Socrates *can* persuade people who refuse to listen. This brief interchange with Polemarchos anticipates Thrasymachos' angry interruption of the discussion of justice. Thrasymachos, like a wild beast, refuses to listen to the discussion and so, according to Glaucon, should not be persuadable. If Socrates had been the observer, he would presumably have recorded the entrance of Thrasymachos as the event which terminated the dialogue and sent him and Glaucon back to Athens. But Socrates knows that Thrasymachos' refusal to listen is really his desire to speak. Since Thrasymachos will not listen to Socrates, Socrates persuades him to listen to himself, i.e., to think about what he is saying. Since (in the language of the *Republic*) justice is more profitable than injustice, no thoughtful man will be unjust. Thinking about what he is saying makes Thrasymachos into a more just man. As a result of Socrates' success in persuading someone who will not listen, we can say that the difference between Socrates and the observer is not between one who irresponsibly thinks he knows the good and so seeks to impose it on others and one who responsibly controls himself from imposing what he does not know. Both Socrates and the observer think the same thing – that it is better to do good than to do bad, that no one should intentionally do bad, that justice is better than injustice. The difference is that Socrates is willing to say and do what he thinks is best while the observer keeps it to himself. By keeping what he thinks to himself, the observer will never discover what Socrates learns from Thrasymachos, namely that Thrasymachos (the unjust man) actually agrees with Socrates and that his bad talk and actions are nothing but a failure to think about what he is saying and doing. Because the observer never says what he thinks, it never occurs to him that Thrasymachos is saying everything without thinking. It is actually the observer's silence which distorts the event that is Thrasymachos' speech because it encourages both of them to persist in the fantasy that Thrasymachos meant what he said. The observer's necessary misunderstanding of Thrasymachos' speech event will become clearer as we formulate in some detail what an observer means by an event.

1

We have said records can be conceived as solutions to the problem of knowledge when the problem takes the form: only the present can be known. Now we take the analysis a step further by grounding this view. How must the world be constituted in order that one could know the present but not the past or future, this place but not other places?

Firstly, the observer's conceptions of time and place imply a conception of things as transient: if what is now need not remain, then the present would be more accessible to an observer than the past or future. Similarly, when what is here need not be there one might be able to have knowledge of this place but not other places. Although these formulations of the observer's version of things are not nearly complete they already begin to show that the observer's versions of time and place rest on or are implicitly views about the nature of things. In other words, the observer's idea of time and place becomes possible when things can be pictured as coming to be and ceasing to be,[8] and passing between here and there. The notion that only the present can be known rests on the basic formulation that what is here need not be there and what is now need not remain.

This is said not to confirm the cliché that 'the world and everything in it is historical . . .',[9] but to launch an examination of how that statement fits with the activity of observation. We have no intention of affirming a factual statement about 'the' world. The view of the world which is characteristic of the observer, i.e., the view that only the present can be known, becomes possible when witnessably extractable things are pictured as being transient and having spatial limitations. By obviating the possibility of omniscience (through his notion that only the present can be known), the observer creates a problem as to what he *can* know, since he cannot, according to his auspices, know all. The observer's work is thus to organize what is extractable and then to bear witness. Omniscience is renounced when the knower is localized in the historicized person and knowledge is localized in historicized time and space. This local character of knowledge as knower and known creates the possibility of mere opinion (as that which reflects the ·historicized person rather than the nature of things), and so establishes also the possibility of observation as a means of coming to terms with the local by extracting through witness. The historicization of knowing grounds the observer as a potential failure (to know). The achievement of adequate observation, hence knowledge, is accomplished by identifying that which is not local (other times, other places) and then extracting from the world that which is local (the present, here).

It has been suggested that the observer's conception that only the present is knowable becomes possible when (1) knowledge is segregated from opinion, and concurrently (2) knowledge is localized. Together they formulate the standard that what is here need not be there and what is now need not remain. However, the historicization of things is not enough to provide for knowledge of the present since while it may suggest why the observer cannot know absent things, it does not indicate why he can know present things. In addition we have been relying on a common-sense, unexplicated version of the present as what an observer can know without defining what an observer's notion of the present is. A deeper formulation is now available: it is not just because what is here need not be there and what is now need not remain that observers can know only the present. More profoundly, the observer's conception of the present is determined by his conception of 'what is', by his conception of events as 'things' with an incorrigibly independent life. Observation, then, presupposes a particular version of things, namely that things have the quality of appearing or showing themselves to those who are present and bear witness when the things appear. It is this quality of things which makes it possible for observers to see them and, in turn, makes possible the observer's version of knowledge: that only the present can be known and that he can know it only by being there. We can now improve on the formulation offered in chapter 2 by noting how it is elliptical to state that observers can know only the present. Observation presupposes a particular way of defining the present, namely not as a moment in time but as a kind of thing – a thing which is presenting itself (to an observer).

If we really do have a deeper version of the observer's version of the present now, we should expect that it will describe what observers do better than the version that observers can know the present in the sense of the present moment. When record-writers, in the role of observers, can claim to know 'the present', they are not referring to a particular point on some abstract continuum of time:

> Hiccups stop – no evidence of continued significant gastrointestinal bleeding. Will be available if needed. Condition stable at present.

> Mrs Sacks is feeling well, she has multiple neurotic complaints, none of which have any bearing on her condition at the present time.

> Patient was sitting in a chair at this time.

> Patient continues sleeping unless disturbed. Less restless now than previously.

In these notes, what can be known is determined by what is showing itself, not by what is current at the moment. In the first note, for example, a claim to know that the hiccoughs have stopped and that there is no bleeding would depend on the claim that these things are not showing themselves. What is appearing is no bleeding and so he who would let things tell him what to say about them, i.e., the observer, can claim there is no 'evidence' of bleeding. That is, what constitutes evidence, what is evident to an observer, is what discloses itself to him without the need for him to participate expect through his presence. The present, in the sense that it is evident to the observer, is not the moment, but the appearing, self-revealing thing. Although these notes do, of course, make use of chronological expressions ('at present', 'at the present time', 'at this time', 'now') observers have surely not decided that it is 'the present instant' or 'now' by looking at a clock and determining that time is passing. Rather, divisions between now and later, past and future, in so far as these divisions differentiate what an observer can know from what he cannot, must be determined by determining what is happening to things. It does not become 'later' for an observer just because a moment passes. As proof of this point, it is not the case that another note becomes necessary when a moment passes. In the fourth note, for example, 'previously' presumably refers not to the previous moment in a clock sense but to a time when *some other thing* (a restless condition) was presenting itself. For an observer, the present in the sense in which he can claim to know it is that time in which something is continuing to disclose itself. It becomes possible for record-writers to know the present, to have a version of 'now', because some thing (the stable condition, the act of sitting, the ability to sleep) is available to be seen by those who would only present themselves.

If the observer conceives of the present not as an instant on the clock, but as the time in which some thing is remaining, it becomes clear why observers can know only the present. They can know only the present because, to them, the present means that which is presenting itself to them. That is, an observer's commitment to the present does not imply a scepticism about 'the next instant'. Rather it implies a commitment to the 'appearance' of things as events which present themselves for observation.

Unlike clock time, there can be no uniformity in the observer's conception of time. If observers define 'the present' by determining whether the thing is remaining, then, depending on how long things are remaining, the present expands and contracts. Thus, in the following notes in which many things are 'happening' there are, as it were, many 'nows':

Self a.m. care. Out of bed and walking around unit most of

day. Disagreeable to all procedures which had to be done. Good appetite at breakfast. At eleven o'clock complains of chills and shaking – did not appear to be severe – would not stay in bed or keep blankets on. Medication given. Refused lunch.

12:30 a.m. Patient moaning very loudly and bringing up vomitus.

1:00 a.m. Patient continues to vomit.

1:15 a.m. Doctor rushed to see patient . . .

1:30 a.m. Patient catherized 30 cc for concentrated urine.

Just as the present time is, for an observer, the *time* during which some thing remains, the present place is the *place* in which some thing is remaining. Places 'belong to the thing itself'.[10] For the observer, place is not a continuum on which are found all conceivable locations. In other words, place is not space. Rather, the observer experiences a different place wherever he experiences a different thing.

The observer's idea of place has been described by Heidegger. What he refers to as the Greek idea of place seems to us to be the observer's concept of place:[11]

That wherein some thing becomes, refers to what we [moderns] call 'space.' The Greeks had no word for 'space.' This is no accident; for they experienced the spatial on the basis not of extension but of place; they experienced it as chora which signifies . . . that which is occupied by what stands there. The place belongs to the thing itself. Each of all the various things has its place.

For an observer to move from one place to another is not merely a matter of his changing spatial co-ordinates, any more than moving from one time to another is a change of chronology. It involves moving from the presence of one thing to the presence of another since, given his conception of place, only things can have places.

Now we can understand more clearly how an observer's kind of presence is possible. Being present is possible because 'the present', in both time and place, is not an abstractly defined set of co-ordinates. Rather, the present is an appearing thing. As such, the concrete kind of presence with it required of observers becomes intelligible. Furthermore, we can now provide for Gottschalk's idea of 'closeness' in time, which puzzled us in chapter 1. One can be close to a time when a time takes the form of an event which is appearing. The record testifies to the witnessing of this appearing and extractable thing.

We can also be clearer now about how the observer's kind of passivity is possible. The observer need not participate or speak since the event is, as it were, doing all the work for him. Since the event is thought to show itself, the observer's job becomes to do, in effect, nothing, so as to let the event show itself. The observer need not speak and so need not expose himself to the contingency of opinion because there is nothing that needs to be disclosed through speech. There is nothing to be disclosed because the relevant thing (events) is disclosing itself. The minimal role left for speech is to remember what has been disclosed after it disappears. Again, speech in the form of records serves not to sustain participation but to sustain non-participation by allowing us to remain silent even in the face of the absent by converting the absent into the permanently present (records). The speech may be different from the event in that it remains but, analytically, what remains as long as the speech remains is the event. So although speech may be different, what makes the difference is not the speech but the event which makes the speech (record) possible.

We must, of course, redraw the boundaries of an observer's knowledge in terms of this version of the present as that which is presenting itself. First there is the possibility of clarifying how an observer stands in relation to knowledge of the present. His claim that he can know the present must not be taken to mean that he knows about the current. Knowing things by observation is not a matter of whether the things are current or not. It is a matter of whether the things are presenting themselves or not. In the following notes record-writers can express ignorance about the chronological present for the simple reason that the chronological present is not showing what it is:

The clinical picture is far from clear. Pleurisy? Periostitis? Myocardial infarction?

Chest clear – epigastric tenderness?

The RAI uptake has been done. Results?

Prosthesis: Unable to obtain info. Patient in coma.

Some aspects of the chronological present remain unclear to these observers: the clinical picture, whether there is epigastric tenderness, what the test results are, and whether the patient has prosthesis. However to argue from these examples to the conclusion that observers cannot know the present is to misunderstand the observer's version of the present. Even in these notes what can be known remains that which is presenting or disclosing itself. In the first note, the observer lets himself be governed by the clinical picture. Since the picture that presents itself is unclear, so is the observer. He will not venture beyond what is presenting itself and so his ignorance affirms rather than denies the observer's rule that only what is present can be known. In all of these notes, the writers continue to follow the observer's rule by letting their speech (record) be guided by the transparent, appearing thing. The observer will speak about that which appears and refuse to speak about that which does not appear. As expressions of knowledge are licensed by the appearance of things so expressions of ignorance (questions, doubt) are licensed by the absence of such an appearance.

It has just been suggested that aspects of the chronological present cannot be known by observers if they do not show themselves. Correlatively, the chronological past and the chronological future *are* potentially knowable by observation if *they* present themselves. Signs, remnants and, we might add, records, are things which, although they may be from the chronological past or future, are within an observer's grasp if they show themselves. It is of course perfectly true that a sign or a remnant may lead an observer to interpret incorrectly the future or the past but it is also true that appearances can be deceiving in the chronological present so the possibility of being wrong does not seem to furnish us with a principle which would allow us to limit observers to the chronological present. What seems to be true in all time-periods is that observers are supposed to limit themselves to what is showing itself rather than to make of the thing 'more' than is there. In the light of this point that observers are not restricted to the chronological present, we can add an additional criticism to the one made earlier concerning Riley's statement that observing is inapplicable to action taking place in the past. It is not just that 'inapplicable' is too weak a word. Now we can see that her view is possibly wrong unless she specifies clearly that by the past she means that which is no longer appearing.

Having shown how the idea that what an observer can know is that which presents itself serves to deepen the idea that observers can know the present, we want next to depict the news contained in the idea that observers can know about things which present themselves by contrasting it with more familiar views. Most accounts of what an observer can know fail to formulate the 'what' at all. We have already quoted Selltiz's vague idea that observers notice 'what is going on around them'. Richardson is equally vague when he writes: 'observers watch, count, listen to and even smell objects or phenomena as they take place.'[12] He has no version of what the 'objects' or 'phenomena' are. It is not just that observers watch phenomena but that the very idea of watching presupposes a particular version of exactly what a phenomenon is: A phenomenon is a thing which reveals itself to him who would only make ready. If all that is required of the observer is making ready so as to let the thing disclose itself, Richardson's grounds for linking watching, listening, counting, and even smelling become clear. If a phenomenon discloses *itself*, then 'seeing' it amounts to merely being able to receive what it gives off. If the purpose is to be such a receptacle, watching, listening, and even smelling would seem to be different ways to do the same job. What all these human faculties have in common is that they are ways of being there without treating one's own being there as anything but a way of taking what is already there. Finally although counting could be formulated as a kind of speaking, it is not so much a contribution to events as a way of disclosing properties already there. In counting, what does not count (what is nothing) is he who makes the count. Hence Richardson is right to connect counting with observing. In counting, as in observing, the fact of one's own speech is not supposed to count.

As a second example of sociological vagueness about the

observer's phenomena, let us consider Goode's characterization of what an observer can know as what is 'out there'.[13] He
gives no formulation of the 'what' that is 'out there' nor of why
this 'what' is located 'out there'. What discloses itself is 'out
there' in the sense that the observer knows, not by participating with the world (i.e., by being a part of it), but by differentiating self and world in order to treat world as that which can
be known and self as that which can do the knowing. The
observer accomplishes this differentiation by treating his own
speech not as part of the world (out there) but as that which
will reflect, as mere product, his contact with the world. For
such unidirectional contact between speech and world to be
possible, the world must be formulated as that which presents
itself and the speech as that which merely captures (records)
the presentation. To say the world is 'out there', then, amounts
to an implicit characterization of the action of observation. The
world is 'out there' to an observer because the observer constitutes himself by refusing to participate, by refusing to treat
his own speech as part of the world. The refusal is possible by
formulating the world, not as including one's participation
through speech, but as that which will be disclosed through
speech.

Both Goode and Richardson fail to describe what an observer
can know because terms like 'out there', and 'phenomenon' are
devoid of content until what observers might mean by these
terms is explicated. Instead of saying that an observer can see
only what is 'there', we say that what an observer conceives of
as 'there' is determined by his grounds. What is there is what
discloses itself without any participation on his part. Unless
what an observer can see is explicated and formulated then
saying that an observer is limited to what is there or to
phenomena amounts to saying that an observer can see what
he can see. Of course he can, but the intellectual task is to
describe what it is that observers can see and not just to repeat
tautologically that they can see what they can see. Our point is
most emphatically not, then, the banal one that observers can
see what is visible. Rather we are trying to characterize exactly
what is visible to an observer. What can an observer see? It is
not just that he can see what is visible but that what is visible
to him is anything which is thought to reveal itself.

2

The observer himself begins to seem strange. The strange thing about the observer's version of visibility as what reveals itself is that there is at least one thing which is not supposed to reveal itself, namely the observer himself. Isn't the observer being unjust by expecting revelations from others when he refuses to make any himself? In terms of this question, the most likely case of injustice in the *Republic* is not Thrasymachos but Glaucon, who expects Socrates to speak about justice without revealing what he himself thinks. Glaucon replaces Thrasymachos as Socrates' main interlocutor for the remaining nine books of the *Republic* but, although he begins with a long account of justice, he tells Socrates that he is presenting not his own views but those of the multitude, namely that as long as one is believed to be just it is more profitable to be unjust than just. Right off, Glaucon sounds like the observer, recording and reproducing the views of others while refraining from saying what he himself thinks. More deeply, Glaucon's very notion of justice proposes that a wise man should not say what he thinks because he could then be unjust without being revealed. The observer as Glaucon represents the good of restraint as concealing his badness from the world. The observer's notion that what is visible is only what reveals itself now amounts to the reassuring belief that if he does not reveal himself no one will learn how bad he is. From Glaucon's point of view, Thrasymachos' mistake is not that he thinks injustice is better than justice but that he does not keep his thoughts to himself.

Socrates interests Glaucon because he seems to be an even better (more restrained, more observant) man than Glaucon himself seems to be. Just as Thrasymachos wants Socrates to listen (permit injustice to be done) Glaucon wants him to speak (loosen his restraints and thus reveal how unjust he actually is). Just as Thrasymachos fails to anticipate that by speaking to Socrates he will also have to listen, Glaucon fails to realize that in order to listen, he will have to speak. Since Socrates will not proceed (speak) without Glaucon's assent, Glaucon is unable to be unjust (keep his secret by not saying what he thinks) while appearing just (agreeing with Socrates) without increasing his own misery (the gap between what he says and what he thinks). Socrates makes him gain conviction: he comes to realize that it is not justice but injustice which causes pain: not what is revealed but what is hidden. The aspect of Glaucon that is visible to Socrates, then, is exactly what the observer claims we cannot see: not what Glaucon presents but what he supposedly hides: the pain that is acting out of the absence of conviction.

Glaucon's pain is another instance of the observer's basic error. As indicated by Glaucon's comical role in the famous discussion of the good, Glaucon thinks the good is pleasure. Socrates is resisting saying what the good is in spite of Adeimantos' requests because he does not know. Glaucon, whose desire for satisfaction (injustice) makes him unwilling to end an enjoyable discussion in which Socrates is doing all the work breaks in with desperate entreaties and readily agrees to Socrates' compromise that only an offspring of the good be discussed. The joke is that in order to obtain the pleasure of further talk Glaucon has to recognize that further talk (pleasure) is not the good but only its offspring. If the good provides pleasure but is not itself pleasure, as Glaucon admits through continuing the discussion, being just (good) will be pleasurable rather than painful. Invisibility as the place where we can escape from the need to do good loses its point if the good pleases us. Glaucon the observer can come to act out of conviction rather than restraint, i.e., he can present himself. Since his notion of not presenting himself (restraint, observation) makes sense only if he mistakenly believes that what pleases him is not good, he is already visible to Socrates anyway.

Socrates always talks to Glaucon as if they were both talking about a third man. At the very point when he is completing the refutation of Glaucon's argument against justice he suggests to Glaucon that they should gently persuade the man who makes such an argument as he does not willingly err, never naming Glaucon himself as the man. The gentleness was also present at the start when Socrates did not demand that Glaucon observe the rules of conversation by presenting his own views rather than those of the multitude. Socrates is gentle because he realizes that Glaucon is afraid of being found

63

out. The gentleness is possible because the point is not to uncover Glaucon's badness but to show Glaucon what is wrong with it. Since badness is an unwilling error, revealing himself to be bad amounts not to the increased pain of public shame but the pleasure that is learning. Seeing he is bad is convincing himself to be good. By not presenting himself, the observer does not just misunderstand Thrasymachos, he also misunderstands himself. The observer could not know what Thrasymachos is thinking but he also cannot know what he himself would say if he dared to speak: he would not reveal his secret, he would lose the need to have one.

3

The vital connection between the idea of an observer, and the idea that things will disclose what must be said about them, can be further illustrated by looking at the connection in terms of the records which are an observer's products. The common conception is that records correspond to the world or that records make selections from the world. Our conception is that it becomes possible for a record to correspond to the world only when 'the world' is formulated as itself revealing the things which must be said about it. This is not to say that the world *does* disclose itself. Rather: in so far as one can formulate the world as made up of things which present or fail to present themselves, it thereby becomes possible for a record to 'represent' the world. It is neither correct or incorrect, then, to treat records as corresponding to the world. The proper statement of the relationship of records to the world is that, in so far as one wants to see records as corresponding to the world, one *must* treat the world as revealing or presenting what must be said about it.

The first point is the most basic: the rule for deciding what can be said in the record is that what can be said must be limited to what is thought to disclose itself. The way the observer denies the contribution of his own speech is by treating his speech as made necessary by 'what has happened', by what is 'revealed to him'. Contrary to conventional methodological accounts, it is too vague to say that what is revealed to an observer is necessarily the 'physical' aspect of things. The 'physical', exactly like the 'mental', may or may not present itself and it is whether some thing presents itself rather than whether some thing is 'physical' which determines whether an observer can see it. The point is that observers are restricted to seeing *all* things in terms of what those things reveal themselves to be. If the 'mental' is thought to disclose itself, then it is just as suitable a topic, then it is just as much within an observer's province, as the 'physical'. Observers do not restrict themselves to the 'physical'. They restrict themselves to the look or appearance of anything (physical, mental, etc.) which is to say they restrict themselves to saying about anything only what that thing makes it necessary for them to say. Even minds, then, are thought of as limits, as bodies in the analytic sense that they control-confine-embody rather than set free.

Those who think observers are limited to 'physical' things[14] might think that these records are observation:

Patient looks more alert and speaks in sentences like 'put it on the table.'

Patient looks well – still has copious purulent drainage from drain site.

Ankles appeared swollen.

whereas these may seem like 'inference':

Patient concerned about forthcoming surgery; about need for private duty nurses.

Comfortable.

Seemed in good spirits.

She tries to be helpful to nurses.

More goal directed than yesterday.

Patient very upset about being in hospital during holiday.

Presumably it would be argued that the second set of examples show that actual record-writers are not 'just' observers. That is, in these records actual record-writers are engaging in two processes: making inferences as well as observations. Note, though, that there is no evidence that the record-writers are more uncertain in the second set of examples than they are in the first. If it is considered noteworthy that the patient only 'seems' to be in good spirits, why is it not equally noteworthy that the ankles only 'appear' to be swollen? Why say that record-writers are inferring in the second set of cases but observing in the first? We say that all of these records are identical in that the observers are letting themselves be guided by what they take to be revealing itself. In all cases, the record-writer's own speech is supposedly produced by what his subject is telling him to say. Of course it is correct that in the first set of cases the *topic* is physical things, whereas in the second set the topic is mental things. However, in both cases the observer writes about a topic by letting his speech be guided by what the thing (ankles on the one hand, spirits on the other) shows itself to be. Observers are not restricted to any one kind of thing but to the treatment of *all* kinds of things as essentially embodying external constraints.

To get the import of the observer's notion that he can and should restrict his speech to what reveals itself, we need to remember how Socrates comes to speak. Socrates is frightened by Thrasymachos but forces himself to speak anyway, tired of talk when Glaucon begins but still ready to grant Glaucon's request. Socrates, unlike the observer, is a speaker and Plato's examples are meant to display what speech is: not self-indulgence (control of mind by body) but self-control (control of body by mind). Socrates speaks, not by revealing, but by controlling his bodily impulses. Since the observer thinks that bodies reveal themselves, he must think that bodies are controlling minds. He is afraid to reveal his mind for the responsible reason that he believes his body is controlling it. He is better than others, the observer is better than the observed, because whereas their minds reveal themselves he manages to control his. The problem arises when we realize that the observer can control his mind only by limiting it to what reveals itself, i.e., only by finding a body which will confine it. What could be learned from this realization is not that we should confine our mind to our bodies but that if we do not control our bodies (our impulses, our fears) our bodies will control (confine) us. Socrates could remind the observer that he need not limit (confine) his speech to what reveals itself since his ability to speak means that he can determine rather than be determined by, control rather than be limited by what reveals itself. Socrates seems to be restricted too in that he is gentle with Glaucon when he could have been harsh and frightened by Thrasymachos without letting himself say so. Yet since it is his notion of the good (his mind) rather than necessity (his body) which generated his restraint, instead of being restricted (confined, limited, the servant of his body) he is doing exactly what he thinks he should. Instead of being embodied by his body, Socrates seeks to create his own limitations, to free himself from what only seem to be limits in order to become author rather than servant of his fate.

Besides the basic issue of what can legitimately be said in a record, other aspects of records are illuminated by the idea that a record reports what discloses itself.

(1) The world must be formulated as telling one what must be said about it for short notes to be able to 'represent' long periods of time:

11:00 – 7:00 Slept well.

11:00 – 7:30 Medication given for sleep. Appears to have slept.

7:00 – 3:30 Had shower. Out of bed walking.

3:00 – 11:30 Continues to improve.

The concept of events makes it possible to treat these records, short as they are, as complete. A phrase like 'slept well' or 'had shower' could represent an entire day if to represent a day means to record what *happened*. Even a short record can be complete if completeness is defined as depending not on the definitiveness of the record but as depending on the simple contingency of whether anything has happened. Thus, by seeing the world as events and making speech depend on events, one has made it possible to say enough without, for example, saying enough to satisfy an audience or solve a problem. Satisfying an audience or solving a problem is incidental in the kind of speech that records exemplify, since one's only standard for what one has to say is what events permit one to say.

In the Socratic dialogues, more seems to happen in a short time than seems possible, e.g., the *Republic* was supposedly spoken in an evening, whereas in the records, less seems to happen than we think possible. Yet the *Republic* does not claim to solve all its problems, e.g., Socrates says his present impulse is not enough to carry him beyond an offspring of the good and we can guess from the behaviour of the disciples in the *Phaedo* that, at the end, Glaucon and the others had not had enough. The observer is afraid that if he begins to speak then, like Socrates, he will run out of time. In order not to face the shortness of a day or a life, by externalizing events he tries not to see how much he can do with them. However, there is at least one day which does not seem too short to Socrates, the day of his death. Crito presents various proposals for extending his life which Socrates declines. Since the cask is empty, he says, it would be foolish to keep drinking. The observer wants to lead a long rather than a full life so his death will bring him up short. The selfsame silence which lengthens his days through the boredom of not speaking when he is able to will resurface in the terrifyingly foreshortened form of death as the experience of wanting to speak without being able to.

(2) Because it is the events which speak, it is even possible for a record to say nothing and yet be adequate. A record-writer can have nothing to say and yet produce an adequate record because it is not he who is thought to be responsible for what is said. What is said is the responsibility of the events and so if nothing happens, then that very absence of anything can be a topic of record:

3:00 – 11:30 No complaints offered.

11:00 – 7:00 Nothing unusual.

7:00 – 3:30 Mrs S. has been quiet all day. Did not verbalize any concerns.

If the world is that which happens and fails to happen and if the observer himself is not thought to be something, it becomes possible to see nothing. Nothing is possible when something is some thing which presents or discloses itself. While it might be said that there is always something in the record, namely the record itself, to make such a point is to forget that from an observer's viewpoint his own speech (record) is supposed to amount to nothing since it is supposed to merely reflect things (or the absence of things) external to itself. In terms of our main theme, these examples provide further insight into why observers think it is good to have nothing to say. From the examples, it is apparent that the observer believes that it is concerns and complaints that patients would verbalize if they were not quiet. The observer probably imagines that his own silence protects others from the stridency he associates with speech. Socrates again becomes relevant since he is a speaker without a complaint. Socrates need not complain even about the event that his death sentence is because no evil can happen to a good man. Instead of death troubling him, death frees him from troubles, i.e., from the need to do good. The observer's mistake is to try to lead a life free from troubles. To the extent that he manages to have his uneventful life he will be unable to welcome his death. His equanimity was only apparent because since he thought it cost him no trouble (thought, speech, conviction) to achieve it, he cannot see the profit in its loss. Hence the stridency, since whereas Socrates need convince only what he can control, i.e., himself, the observer needs to control what he can't convince, i.e., the true indifference that is death. Unlike his death, the observer could respond to Socrates with equanimity because Socrates is not trying to control (kill) him but to encourage him to take control of himself. The observer would not lose his healthy concern about death but he would become able to speak about it: his concern would be transformed from the private complaint that we have to die to the public conviction that we should live well. Instead of troubling himself about his death, he could trouble others with the good example of his life.

(3) Finally, we shall differentiate our account of the record-event link from that given by Labov and Waletsky in their analysis of narratives. They define a narrative as a 'method of recapitulating past experiences by matching of the verbal sequence of clauses to the sequence of events which actually occurred'.[15] They might say that the following note is a narrative because it 'recapitulates experience in the same order as the original event'[16]:

Patient had cardiac arrest. Immediate cardio-pulmonary resuscitative measures instituted but failed to revive the patient. Patient pronounced dead at 10:56 p.m. on 9/28/69.

By making the important issue whether the clauses of the account have the same time order as the original events, they presuppose too much. How *can* a set of sentences have a time order, for example? Perhaps they would say this is possible because the sentences refer back to the events, but exactly what does that mean? They must describe how one thing (a sentence) can refer back to (recapitulate) another thing (events). This is the issue we focus on. A narrative is possible in so far as things (events) are thought to disclose themselves. Therefore, speech can be thought of not as adding some thing but as repeating what is there. Speech can repeat a thing if a speech need not be thought of as itself a thing but can be 'about' other things. This view of speech is accomplished by ridding speech of any contribution except the contribution of making a record. The sameness of narrative and event is not adequately described as a matching of order of sentences in the report to order of events. The narrative is the same as the event in the more fundamental sense that it *is* the event, since the narrative is supposed to be nothing but a disclosure of what has already been experienced. Events are 'original' not just in Labov and Waletsky's narrow sense that they happened first but in the sense that events are thought to originate, that is, produce, the speech about them, thus making the happening that is speech not itself original but a repeat.

Although narrative seems to be a product of experience, the very impulse to recapitulate shows that one who is limited to narrative has not had the decisive experience, namely the experience of the good (aporia). If he had had that experience, since his speech and actions would be informed by it, he would not feel the need to match his speech to it. Instead of recapitulating or disclosing his past experiences by speaking about them, his experience would be re-presented or exemplified in everything he says and does. At first glance the *Republic* looks like a narrative: it is apparently a recapitulation by Socrates of the events of the previous day. Yet although Socrates is speaking it was of course Plato who wrote the story, so it is not a recapitulation but an imitation of Socrates. Listening to Socrates must have involved the experience of wanting to be like him. Instead of referring back to this experience, Plato continues to have it by seeking to write as if he were Socrates. Socrates, as we know, was not a writer but a speaker. As just one instance of his commitment to the good rather than his own originality, then, Socrates risked not having his story told. Plato's way of rescuing Socrates from oblivion is not to repeat his story but to re-present the same risk: by impersonating Socrates and not disclosing his own role in the story he is showing the selfsame commitment by risking that his own contribution will never be noticed.

The observer shares Socrates' and Plato's healthy reluctance for the sheer originality that is telling one's own story. Yet instead of *risking* that his story will not be told by basing it on a presupposition that he cannot himself disclose or be sure others will see (the good), the observer *ensures* that his story will not be told by stifling himself and telling others' stories instead. The observer needs to see that Socrates' willingness to speak (and Plato's to write) are not irresponsible because instead of defining or disclosing the good, they depend on it. Socrates neither formulates himself (like the others to whom the observer is forced to listen) nor formulates others (like the observer) but as it were invites the good to formulate both him and others. Instead of either a narrator or a self-disclosing event we have someone who risks a life which cannot be repeated but only exemplified or re-presented and which therefore remains inaccessible to us as long as and in so far as the good remains inaccessible to us. The observer's aporia will come when he risks presenting himself (speaking, writing). He will discover that his fears of imposing himself on the world are groundless. He will discover that the others will *still* not tell his story though a few may begin to imitate him. He will see that what differentiates him from the multitude is not (as he believes) his restraint but (as Plato and Socrates can see) his commitment to the good.

4

In the final section of this chapter, we shall note an implication of the connection between events and observation. The grounds of observing and recording, as we have formulated them, make it necessary that observers see only one thing at a time. Of course, the notion that observers cannot see two things at once has been available for some time in psychologically orientated discussions of 'attention'. Edwin Boring writes:[17]

> There really is a fundamental fact of attention. The fact of attention is that consciousness is limited. Attention to one 'thing' requires inattention to others. If you are paying attention to the old lady in the pew in front of you, presumably you are not paying attention to the sermon.

Vernon writes:[18]

> It seems possible that we cannot attend to two events happening at one and the same moment, and perceive both of them clearly. Thus it was found that it was impossible to take in two pieces of information presented simultaneously, one visually and the other aurally . . . unless the two events can be combined in some way, one must be overlooked.

To explain why observers can see only one thing at a time, the psychologists resort to physiological facts. Thus, Boring believes that:[19]

> At a given moment a person can think of so much and no more because he has just so much brain with which to do the thinking. . . .

As Sanders describes it, the single-channel theory states: 'that while processing one signal, one is blocked for others.'[20] Unlike the psychologists, we will not rest our argument that the observer can see only one thing at a time on physiological grounds. Rather, the key question for us to examine is how the observer's knowledge organizes his attention: (1) what is an observer's conception of a thing? (2) what is an observer's conception of 'at a time'?

Answers to these questions are implicit in our previous discussion. An observer conceives of a thing as an event. Psychologists who try to account for 'one-at-a-time' while using the furniture of material objects as their 'thing', are missing the essential point that, for an observer, these objects are not things.[21] Rather, events are things. If an event and not just an ordinary object is, for an observer, a thing, then the question of the possibility of 'one-at-a-time' becomes transformed. It is no longer a question of the observer's physiological ability to hold two objects in focus at once. It is a question of whether, given the socially organized nature of events and observers, this nature would enable one observer to see two *events* at once.

To decide this issue, we must move to a second question: what is an observer's conception of 'at once'? As was suggested in section 1, an observer's idea of 'at once' is not determined by looking at a clock or map. An observer decides that it is 'now' rather than later because some thing is continuing to 'happen'. He decides that it is 'later' when some other thing begins to happen.[22] In other words, an observer's idea of what time it is is dependent on his idea of what is happening. He will see the time as the present, as now, as long as he continues to see one thing happen. When he sees another thing happen, he will see the time as 'later'. Thus it is inconceivable that an observer can see two things at once not because of physiological limitation but because the observer's idea of 'at once' requires that he see only one thing. Whenever he sees two things, he will also see two times since, for him, the idea of two times requires the fact of two things. For an observer, the idea of two things at one time is analytically inconceivable.

It should be noted that we are *not* saying, as do Gestalt and other psychologists, that observers tend to unify their diverse perceptions.[23] It is not a matter of perception at all. We are saying that whatever observers see as one thing they will also see as one time. One-at-a-time is not necessary for observation as a consequence of the simultaneous perception of wholes in parts; the necessity of one-at-a-time resides instead in the identity of one thing with one time.

Exactly the same point can be made with regard to place. The observer cannot see two things in one place because the idea that he is seeing one thing, means that he is also in one place. His idea that he is seeing two things would force him to conceive of himself as in two places.

As we have already noted, Socrates' answer to the observer's fear of definitive speech is to recommend dialogue, i.e., two-at-a-time. In terms of our current topic, it seems as if Socrates is either asking us to rack our brains irresponsibly as the physiologists would fear, or setting the analytically impossible requirement that we be in two places or times at once. To assess these criticisms, we need a Socratic sense of time and place. During his *Apology*, Socrates says that what he has done with his life is his lot, what it has been allotted to him to do. Time and place would not be what he, like the observer's events, takes up but what he has already been given, the space within which he is to do his work. The refusal to escape from Athens and to delay drinking the poison mean not taking up others' time and place, i.e., not making others wait until later or move somewhere else, but taking only the portion of time and place, i.e., the fate, that is already his. Similarly, the criticism of the accusers is that they are hurting themselves. Their thoughtlessness amounts not to cutting short *his* time but to not taking their own time. Socrates and the accusers need not be two separate and competing ones who would confuse each other's brains or fight for time and place. The implication is that though Plato's and Socrates' preferred mode, dialogue, is two-at-a-time, the two should be thought of not as two ones but as parts of the whole. Dialogue provides an instance of two who, though different, are deeply at one with each other. Socrates' reluctant speaking and Glaucon's eager listening show how the one who has seen the good and knows it cannot be formulated could talk to the one who desperately wants to see it: how a good teacher should relate to a good student. Similarly Plato's stories of Socrates show how a writer could be true to the selfsame impulse that made a speaker speak. Asking the observer to participate in dialogue, then, is not asking the observer to do more than he can but to do exactly what he can: not to be two ones but to be someone, to play his part in the whole.

Part Two

Implications of the Grounds of Records for the Uses of Records

4 Reliability

In earlier chapters we have been concerned with the grounds of the activity of recording. Now we shift our focus to the uses of records. However, the grounds of records and the uses of records are not the different issues they may appear to be since what makes records possible provides for and delimits the uses to which records may be put. Furthermore, even the fact that records are the kind of thing which it is appropriate and possible to *use* will be shown to be a consequence of the grounds of records. We shall find, then, that the various concerns connected with the use of records can be understood as another manifestation of the grounds of the activity of recording. The analysis to be done now will serve to justify further our point that it is necessary to provide the basic grounds of records since it will be shown that a successful analysis of the uses of records requires reference to the grounds of the activity of recording. We begin our discussion of how records are used with a characterization of those who are important users of medical records – bureaucrats.

1

The distinction between opinion and knowledge and the consequent desire to control speech, which ground the observer's interest in presence, find derivative expression in the bureaucratic concern with appearance (the recorded record) and reality (the truth of the recorded record). In each case, the recognition of the contingent or conventional character of speech – its problematic adequacy with regard to whether it is faithful to the event which it is about – gives rise to the attempt to void this contingency by voiding any participation through speech in the recording of the event.

The difficulty with presence as a solution to the problem of knowledge is that records are used by persons who are not present. Consequently, the user is faced with the question of how to reachieve in his use the purity of the original record in the face of (1) his absence at the point when the event has presented itself and (2) his own capacity to contaminate the record by participating through speech. The user's problem of imperfect or incomplete speech is the same as the observer's (they are members of the same knowledge-opinion community). Potentially the user shares the observer's remedy of eliminating the problem by eliminating the speech which equivocates the nature of the event. However, the user is confronted with a special difficulty as a result of the observer's way of solving the problem: how is the user supposed to achieve the silence necessary for him to be able to listen to the record? How might he resolve the problem of participant speech, when the opportunity to accomplish this through presence is by definition closed to him? In a way, all bureaucracy can be seen as an attempt to create a method for the reduction of contingency, imperfection, and error, an attempt which is re-presented in the bureaucrat-as-user's effort to reduce his participation in the reading of the record.

It should be noted that we are not discussing isolated instances in which records are patently erroneous or flawed, or where administrators explicitly address standards of record-keeping. The point is that the very *possibility* of a record emanates from a conception of speech as conventional, dangerous, and opinionated, and the concomitant attempt to forestall this human danger by the creation of a circumstance in which knowledge can be received as a gift from the events which are thought to be the source and substance of knowledge. This is to say, then, that every record displays the abiding observational-bureaucratic concern regarding the contamination of the record through participant speech. Given that records *are* speech, of course, and therefore only contingently adequate, it is the bureaucrat's job as a user of records to continuously and assiduously repair each and every instance of the contingency which records inevitably are. It is of course true that administrators (like sociologists) find some records more adequate than others. However, our point is that every such finding (whether of adequacy or inadequacy), presupposes a solution to the basic problem of achieving a relationship to records, a solution which does not involve speaking to and hence contaminating the record in spite of the fact that being absent at the original event, administrators are seemingly unable to decide whether records are adequate or not.

Generally, then, the bureaucrat sees the record's speech (since it is speech) as potentially unreal, as no more than an appearance. In a variety of ways which we shall specify in detail, bureaucratic work consists of remedying the contingency of the record by regenerating bureaucratic speech as a technical matter in the service of the events which are real. For example, as we shall show, bureaucrats try to conceive of their speech as generated by records in the same way that observers treat their speech as generated by events. In addition, as we shall show, bureaucrats try to subject their speech to events by formulating themselves as subject to observers. By making speech secondary, artificial, and only technically necessary, the bureaucrat makes his speech subservient to that which it is about. If the user asks himself how to preserve the record from contamination, he can produce an answer by reorganizing the idea of speech from that which originates to that which follows, in this case that which follows from records.

The bureaucrat prevents himself from speaking by making his speech into a thing at the disposal of its subject. We might express this point by saying that the bureaucrat's problem is to be able to *use* the record. It sounds banal, perhaps, but now we are in a position to understand better what the idea of using means. It means to be able to establish the kind of relationship in which ego (bureaucrat) can conceive of alter (record) as an object which, like a ripe apple, is there for the picking. To *use* some thing is to treat it as self-sufficient, finished, and so available for the relationship we call use rather than the relationship we call participation. To treat something as use-able is to be able to stop thinking (speaking) about it. The bureaucrat's problem is that he must somehow achieve this using relationship with records even though, through his absence, the record has seemingly become a questionable thing. The bureaucrat must somehow move from questioning (speaking to, participating with) records to listening to records. The bureaucrat must listen to the record so that the only speech which ensues becomes the exclusive domain of the record. One can understand the exasperation of administrators as listeners, listeners who are devoted to certain standards (of reality in our case) but who cannot control the performances (records) which are measured in terms of these standards. What appears (the record) may not be real (the event), and the bureaucrat is without the resource (presence) to decide.

Their exasperation reveals that they exemplify a perennial possibility, albeit in a modern guise. Thus, they remind us of the soul in Plato's Myth of Er who chose a horrible life and then proceeded to blame fate and heaven and anything but himself for his fate. Exasperation, then, is a superficial response by the bureaucrats because it seeks to avoid understanding how they have inflicted their situation on themselves by refusing to say what they think. Their exasperation amounts to choosing to avoid the pain of saying what they think in just the way the soul in the myth seeks to avoid a hard choice and ends up with a horrible life. Our point to bureaucratic types is not that opinions are not hard but that they cannot be avoided since if they are not expressed initially they will resurface anyway in the form of exasperation. Expressing them initially is better because then at least one knows exactly what is hard, i.e., the discrepancy between opinion and reality, between one's fate and what would satisfy one and *not* the fact that others are opinionated as well, not anything but the way we are. If the bureaucrat could understand this point, he might find his life less hard in the sense that instead of imagining that he has no opinions and endlessly discovering that he does he would be facing the fact that he has opinions and hence could begin to get rid of them, not by suppressing but by expressing them. In terms of the myth, instead of the bad trip into exasperation and worse that goes with the oblivion of those who forget their nature, he could have the wisdom which will permit him to face with good cheer what he has to go through anyway.

2

In this chapter and the next we shall try to describe in detail some of the ways in which bureaucrats subjugate their speech to the record. We shall begin with the observation that bureaucratic control requires supervision. That is to say, by refusing to be opinionated, the higher orders lose the ability to rule in the Socratic sense of saying and doing what they think best for the whole and relegate themselves to just watching over the others. However, even from a modern perspective this supervisory requirement is problematic when it is applied to the activity of record-keeping since it raises the question of how supervision of record-making can be conducted in such a way that it is consistent with the ideal of speechlessness. How can the bureaucrat supervise without deciding, participating, and speaking and how can he speak when, being absent at the original event, his speech would not be controlled?

Many writers have, of course, identified supervision as a major feature of bureaucracy. As Weber writes:[1]

> The principles of office hierarchy and of levels of graded authority mean a firmly ordered system of super- and subordination in which there is a supervision of the lower offices by the higher ones.

Etzioni, too, emphasizes the fact that bureaucratic structures require supervision:[2]

> Most organizations most of the time cannot rely on most of their participants to carry out their assignments voluntarily. . . . The participants need to be supervised, the supervisors themselves need supervision, and so on, all the way to the top of the organization. In this sense, the organizational structure is one of control, and the hierarchy of control is the most central element of the organizational structure.

Like supervision, record-keeping is an important element of bureaucratic organization. Weber writes:[3]

> The management of the modern office is based upon written documents ('the files') which are preserved in their original or draught form.

Furthermore, researchers have often looked at the relationship between these two facets of bureaucracy. Blau has shown how records play an important role in the supervisory process.[4] Erikson and Gilbertson suggest that medical records can be used by supervisors and others in order to evaluate personnel:[5]

> The dossier is not only a record of a particular patient; it is a record of the personnel who have contributed materials to it and a record of the institution. Among the most interested consumers of dossiers, then, are administrators trying to monitor operations of the plant, teachers trying to measure the progress of students, attorneys trying to keep informed about legal difficulties, supervisors trying to evaluate the performance of the staff, researchers engaged in a variety of investigations and so on.

What is being said here? How can a record be a record of its maker rather than its subject, and why would this kind of record interest an administrator? Originally, we had the event and only the event speaking to us. Now we come upon the possibility that the recorder is also making an appearance as the maker of the record, which raises a question about the relation of this to our first formulation (presented in chapters 1, 2, and 3) that the event is the sole participant (analytically) and so the record is not a record of the recorder. It remains to work through the Erikson and Gilbertson phrase 'record of the institution' to show how it is another instance of the knowledge-opinion distinction, and so is compatible with our earlier formulation. To anticipate, treating a record as a record of the institution will turn out to be an administrator's way of using the record given (1) his absence at the original event and (2) his commitment to non-participation. That is, the administrator converts the record into the maker's record in order to make it subject to a kind of supervision which will not require participation.

It is undoubtedly true, as Blau and Erikson and Gilbertson note, that supervisors can use records to evaluate personnel. However, a prior aspect of the relationship between supervision and record-keeping is that, for the bureaucrat who was not present, record-keeping surfaces as a phenomenon which poses for him the bureaucrat-as-user's problem: how to assert and then solve the appearance-reality, knowledge-opinion distinction. The bureaucrat looks to some method for achieving the distinction in order that his (institutional) use of the record can be controlled by that method. Perhaps his use can be controlled by his controlling the recorder – in effect by his becoming the observer. As we shall explicate below, supervising the recorder may be a method for bringing the bureaucrat to the event by achieving analytic identity with the recorder. We shall examine this possibility as a more rigorous formulation of the conventional sociological statement that in bureaucracies the functions of supervision and record-keeping are paramount.

We launch our investigation of the supervision-record user link by considering an obvious requirement of supervision. Merton has pointed out that 'visibility of both norms and of role-performance is required if the structure of authority is to operate effectively.'[6] Moreover:[7]

> effective and stable authority involves the functional requirement of fairly full information about the actual (not the assumed) norms of the group and the actual (not the assumed) role-performance of its members.

Merton is writing about the behaviour of persons, including persons who make and keep records. To achieve the appearance-reality distinction the bureaucrat has to organize it with regard to the production of records, which is to say that for the bureaucrat to 'know' rather than 'opine' he needs to generate a collection of actions which will reproduce the knowledge that is potential in the record. In common parlance: what would an administrator have to know to evaluate a record? Given the obvious purpose of records, i.e., to represent events, in order to decide whether a record was adequate, an administrator would presumably have to decide whether it was true. Administrators must determine whether what the record reported has, in fact, happened.

As has been emphasized, however, the idea of recording requires that only those who are present can know what happened. Thus, in so far as they are committed to the grounds which make it reasonable to record, supervisors can never *know* whether a given record is true. Those who were not present cannot know what happened and cannot evaluate records in terms of their accuracy without (1) ignoring the very basis of their whole enterprise or (2) transforming the idea of presence so as to warrant a different but faithful sense of knowledge. While it would be simple for us to opt for the first option and so write off bureaucracy as just another case of self-contradictory group behaviour, a careful examination reveals that bureaucracy generates a coherent and complementary display of ground and action.

Because the administrators' ignorance is structurally determined, it would seem to be an irremediable aspect of the record-keeping system. Although Blau and Scott state that administrators 'seek to widen the sphere of [their] influence over employees beyond the controlling power that rests on the legal contract or formal sanctions',[8] administrators could not extend their range of control to include the assessment of the truth of records without violating the basic principle that only presence leads to knowledge. This is not necessarily to disagree with Blau and Scott, but it is to suggest that their statement is too sanguine. Even granting the administrator's *desire* to widen his sphere, we would want to know *how* it is possible for him to include within his sphere even such a bureaucratically ordinary object as a record since his absence would seem to make any influence or control on his part unwarranted. In addition, if it is true that bureaucrats seek to 'influence' record-keeping, the nature of such influence remains to be specified since the very idea of influence seems to go against the concept of a record as independently produced by events. Most basically, by looking at how they handle their dilemma can we come up with a more informative version of what bureaucrats desire?

3

Two responses to the problem will be discussed in detail. (1) Administrators try to assess records indirectly by concerning themselves with the 'reliability' of record-writers. (2) When administrators do assess records directly, they try to assess them in terms of *completeness* rather than truth.[9]

The first solution seeks to sustain the fundamental tenet that non-observers cannot know what happened and observers can, while simultaneously rejecting the possible consequence that non-observers are ignorant concerning what happened.

Instead of assuming the posture of ignorance, non-observers can see themselves as *depending upon* or relying on observers. Relying on observers is a device for making it possible that non-observers know what has happened, without at the same time violating the idea that, *qua* non-observers, they should be incapable of such knowledge. By being able to 'rely', non-observers make it unnecessary that they remain ignorant even though they were not present. At the same time, they are not violating the idea that only presence can lead to knowledge. The fact that they must *rely on* observers rather than know 'on their own' is an acknowledgment of the principle that only presence can lead to knowledge.

The more general point is that non-observers are put in the position of having to rely on observers because of the grounds of the activity of observing. Given that only those who are present can know what happened, unless non-observers can rely on observers, only events which had been personally observed could be known. Thus, unless knowledge is to take a bureaucratically useless form, the basic idea that observing depends on presence requires the complementary idea that non-observers can rely on observers.

Reliability effectively achieves bureaucratic presence by negating the difference between the one who records and the one who uses the record. The interaction which is reliability reaffirms a commitment to distinguishing between presence and absence and hence between knowledge and opinion, but it achieves this reaffirmation by re-presenting the observer and bureaucrat as analytically identical, such that the real can make its appearance equally to observer and bureaucrat. The *action* they are to do is different: the observer observes, the bureaucrat uses; the observer records, the bureaucrat supervises; the observer works to get into position, the bureaucrat to control. But these differences in action are generated by the shared commitment to the difference between knowledge and opinion and the shared commitment to attaining knowledge by refusing to speak so as to let the event disclose itself. The reliability of the observer, in which he becomes an extension of the bureaucrat's outer reach, thus brings the bureaucrat to the event and dissolves the problem of presence-absence while maintaining the distinction which had originally made it a problem. Such a formulation enlivens and deepens the notions of interdependence and division of labour, terms which are so common but unexamined in the literature on organizations. If bureaucrat and observer form a division of labour, we can note that what is decisive about the division is not that they have two different jobs but that they go about doing the same basic job (not participating) in different ways, the one by relying, the other by being reliable. Focus on their differences would thus be deceptive since it would hide the fact that their differences are produced by a shared commitment. As for 'interdependence' it is doubtful that that is an adequate term to characterize the observer-administrator relationship made possible by the idea of reliability. First of all, interdependence probably suggests some sort of symmetry whereas in this case, instead of both depending, the one depends while the other must be dependable. Second, rather than interdependence, their relationship is better characterized as one of identity since it is analytic identity which they produce through relying and being rely-able. The administrator does not just depend on the observer, he *becomes* the observer by being able to rely on him.

It has been suggested that the possibility of relying on observers allows non-observers to know about events they have not witnessed without violating the principle that knowledge can be obtained only by those who are present. Bureaucrats bring the possibility into being by the method of controlling observers through the grammar of evaluation. Non-observers can and do convert the fact that they are relying on observers into a method of evaluation. Instead of deciding whether records are true, non-observers can decide (discuss) whether record-writers are 'rely-able'. The bureaucrat changes the topic from record to record-keeper, a move which is perfectly consistent with the notion that he can know through relying. By making the observer into the topic, he gives himself licence to speak. He can speak because his topic is not what happened. His topic is his attempt to control those who let him know what happened. With his new topic, everything he says, every attempt to exercise control over observers, is not an expression of his independence and therefore a contaminating influence on the event. Rather, the administrator's speech expresses his dependence on the observer and therefore the event. Speech about reliability, which we shall show to be so characteristic of administrators, emerges as a clear-cut example of the point made earlier that the administrator, like the observer, attempts to subject his speech to the event. The bureaucrat wants a method for controlling speech, i.e., he wants a method which is not speech. How can he achieve this speechlessness? Although concretely the administrator is talking, by talking about observer reliability, his *message* is that he is submitting his speech to the sovereignty of he who can know, and he is identifying the knower as he who can afford to be silent because the event tells him what to say. The administrator is saying that he can only know through relying and therefore that the source of his knowledge is not his own speech but the observer's speech and, ultimately, the event which permits the observer to speak.

What is being offered here is a new formulation of a well-known fact: whenever observation is used as a means of obtaining knowledge, the reliability of observations becomes an issue. Almost all discussions about observation or recording mention the problem of reliability. For example, Selltiz writes that 'A good measurement procedure must be . . . reliable.'[10] Cannel and Kahn write:[11]

> Scarcely less important than validity is reliability, which has to do with the stability and equivalence of a measure.

Weick:[12]

> Observational methods are more vulnerable to the fallibilities of human perceivers than almost any other method.

And Nagel:[13]

> the undeniable difficulties that stand in the way of obtaining reliable knowledge of human affairs because of the fact that social scientists differ in their value orientations are practical difficulties.

Taking Nagel's assertion seriously, we might wonder why, if the difficulties are practical, they are also 'undeniable'. If the difficulties can be remedied practically why don't they just go away? When Nagel says that reliability is a practical difficulty, we would formulate the practicality as the fact that the difficulty is remedied through practices, namely the practice which, from the perspective of users involves relying and from the perspective of observers involves being reliable. Strictly speaking, then, what is practical, i.e., something to be done, is the solution represented in the idea of relying but the difficulty is not practical; the difficulty is what makes the practice necessary. Furthermore, the difficulty is not adequately formulated as some thing standing in the way of reliable knowledge since the basic difficulty (the fact that non-observers, being absent, cannot know) has been solved, albeit practically, with the acknowledgment implicit in Nagel that relying can be a method of knowing. By not focusing on his own implicit acknowledgment, Nagel obscures the fact that the difficulty has been solved, not by the practices, but by the decision to let relying be a way of knowing, i.e., by the decision which makes the practices necessary.

What is lacking in most[14] discussions of the issue of reliability is an understanding of *why* reliability becomes an issue whenever observation and recording are used as means of obtaining knowledge. The concern with reliability arises because of the fundamental fact that opinionated non-observers are relying on knowledgeable observers to convert themselves into knowledgeable users. When Cannel and Kahn write of reliability as the 'equivalence of a measure', we would reformulate it as the equivalence of observer and user. This is to say that the measure, as reliability, is the degree of analytic identity between recorder and bureaucrat, an identity which universalizes the event without at the same time contaminating it by opinionated bureaucratic participation. The bureaucrat does not have to fuss with the record itself as long as he controls the observer and thereby has contact with the observation. Only because non-observers are in the position of relying on observers does observers' reliability become a possible question. Given the fact that observers are being relied on, obviously it will become relevant to decide whether they are, in fact, 'rely-able'. The concern with reliability is, then, nothing but a user's way of expressing the essential suspicion of participation in the event.

Our account of reliability must be carefully distinguished from others' accounts. We are *not* saying that a concern with reliability arises because 'humans are fallible',[15] 'social scientists differ in their value orientations',[16] or 'our sense organs operate in a highly variable, erratic, and selective manner.'[17] Even if we were inclined to accept all these assertions, they would not tell us why reliability becomes an issue in the first place. That humans are fallible does not explain why human failures matter to record-users. That social scientists differ does not explain why such differences constitute a problem. Finally, the supposed properties of our sense organs do not explain why we should be concerned about such properties. To explain why reliability becomes an issue is not to cite the 'defects' which make for unreliability since these defects are formulated as defects only because there has been a decision to make reliability matter. Therefore, we need to ask why the question of reliability even arises. It arises from the selfsame commitment to the activity of observing which reliability resolves. The concern with reliability is a practical expression of the basic fact that the absent non-observer's structural position is always and irremediably one of dependence in a world where the truth resides in the local nature of immediate events.

Other attempts to explain why troubles arise over reliability are too superficial. Roth's description of information flow in a hospital can serve as an example:[18]

> The [medical] staff often has difficulty obtaining reliable information about the patient, partly because some kinds of information by their very nature resist definition and measurement, and partly because of the manipulation of information by patients and various staff groups.

It is undoubtedly true that patients and staff groups manipulate information and that some information is resistant to measurement. However, these facts alone cannot explain why the staff has difficulty obtaining reliable information since to merely cite these facts is to presuppose without explicating why they might be relevant. A full explanation of the staff difficulties would require that Roth note that reliability becomes a difficulty only because the staff must simultaneously generate and overcome the difference between themselves, on the one hand, and patients and staff, on the other hand, as users and observers. They generate the differences by committing themselves to observation without being present. They overcome the differences by relying. The staff must rely on patients and staff groups for its information, i.e., work to achieve analytic identity with them, because of the very nature of the activity of observing. Roth's account gives the impression that the difficulties over reliability come from contingent features of this particular organization. However, these particular features are noteworthy to organization members and to Roth only because of the matter which he leaves unexplicated: the essential character of the activities of observing and using.

To be blunter still, it is the supervisor who has generated the problem with which this chapter is concerned by his decision to rely which is really the decision to supervise (watch over without participating) rather than rule. Contrary to Roth, Nagel, and the rest, what is needed to truly solve his problem is another version of the relation between the present and the absent besides the supervisory one. Whereas supervisory types have an active desire to be present everywhere and treat facts of time and place as unfortunate contingencies, by the time he died Socrates actually wanted to absent himself even from his best friends. Whereas the supervisor wishes he could rely on everyone (know everything), Socrates apparently will not even let anyone rely on him. Because he is just expressing his opinions, Socrates knows that he is unreliable even if he is present. Hence his desire for dialogue as an attempt to discover whether anyone else has the knowledge he knows he lacks and eventually his desire for death as release from a state in which he knows he cannot know. Socrates' life consists in expressing his opinions while facing the fact that he does not know if what he says is true and his death provides him with his reward: not having to speak anymore about what he does not know. The irony is that Socrates' sense of what his opinions lack makes them the most reliable of which men are capable: Socrates would make the best ruler because he is so reluctant to undertake the task. If Socrates represents rule by the best, bureaucracy represents rule by no one (its version of reliability). Those who are naturally the best (the supervisors?) are blind to the irony in their position and so withhold the opinions which Socrates reluctantly expresses. The ironic (frustrating) result is rule by those who feel no such reluctance, i.e., the worst. Hence the very need to supervise which presupposes enmity between the 'lower' and 'higher' order. Instead of supervising those who are 'lower', thereby making them desire his absence, Socrates works for them (rules), thereby instilling in them the desire for his permanent presence. Socrates, who wishes he can absent himself, is always being asked by the others to remain while the supervisor, who wants to be present everywhere, is a *persona non grata* – everyone wishes he would leave. The difference on the personal level is that Socrates gets his wish eventually – he is saved, whereas the supervisor is perennially frustrated – he is doomed. And in terms of effectiveness, we suggest below that none of the supervisor's efforts (control) serve to make the others any better than they would otherwise be.

4

Instead of evaluating *records*, administrators can concentrate their efforts on attempting to ensure the reliability of record-*keepers*. Administrators can use the following logic: although the truth of records cannot be directly determined, records are true to the extent that record-keepers are reliable. Therefore, by attempting to make record-keepers reliable, they are indirectly attempting to make records truthful. They can assert their supervisory prerogative, not by watching over records but by watching over observers. In the rest of this chapter, we shall present evidence to suggest that although administrators and clerks do not directly assess the truth of records (since that is impossible), they devote considerable administrative energy to ensuring the reliability of record-keepers.

Several ways in which the administration tries to supervise record-keeping by fostering the reliability of record-keepers will be discussed: (1) restricting the 'privilege' of record-writing to professionals and semi-professionals. (2) Imposing legal and other kinds of sanctions on record-writers. (3) Instituting review procedures, and (4) making bureaucratic tasks concurrent with medical tasks. In true bureaucratic fashion, these methods merely re-present the problem.

(1) *Professional reliability*

Most students of the professions stress that doctors acquire freedom from control in return for high commitment to the norm of responsibility:[19]

> the very great prestige of the professions is a response of the society to their apparent self denial, i.e., they can, but typically do not, exploit.

Goss writes:[20]

> Physicians place high value on assuming personal responsibility and exercising individual authority in making professional decisions. Accordingly, their role expectations emphasize independence in the realm of professional work.

Whatever other purposes it serves, the fact that only professionals and 'semi-professionals' (nurses, social workers, etc.) may write in the record can be seen as an administrative tactic to encourage dependable record-keeping. Only those who could be expected to be reliable, because of their professional commitments, are permitted to make entries in the medical record.

Some semi-professionals are very proud of the fact that they may write in the record. When asked to differentiate herself from recreation workers, an occupational therapist noted that recreation workers had no access to the medical record. Writers proud of the privilege of writing records should be less likely to abuse the privilege. We are not, of course, insisting on the empirical point that professionals and semi-professionals will produce more reliable records than untrained clerks. We are saying that the idea of restricting the record to doctors and other 'trustworthy' types, whether it works or not, shows bureaucratic recognition that record users must trust record-writers in order to achieve analytic identity with them. Here is a very concrete demonstration of Goode's point about professional self-denial. It is not just that professionals work for low wages but that in an actual situation when self-denial, i.e., control over desire so that the event may be permitted to speak, is called for, professionals are being asked to do the job.

The trouble is that professional reliability does not amount to knowledge but opinion so reliance on professionals has the usual frustrating result. The supervisor expects them to relieve him of his absence. The professionals respond as they do to any pain. They either comfort him:

Dr Erix notified and responded immediately.

Husband refuses bloodletting after careful explanation.

Rushed to operating room.

Made as comfortable as possible.

With Mrs Colam's permission, I telephoned on 11/5.

or seek to cure him through some opinionated intervention of their own:

The most likely site of bleeding is, of course, marginal ulcer.

This patient is not likely to recover any cerebral functioning. She was functioning marginally before accident. I would therefore strongly object to any heroics.

The prognosis without surgery is practically nil for an improved function state; with surgery the risk is very high. The decision for surgery is therefore made with the utmost reluctance.

Patient noted 5 Grand Mal seizures in last 3 months. I know she can be controlled at levels which produce sedation.

There is nothing surgical to offer

When a patient is discharged too early from a strictly medical viewpoint in order to attend a circumcision:

Free of pain – because of noise and sick patients in room and patient's extreme excitement I feel he will do better at home and therefore discharged today.

Instead of knowledge, the supervisor gets treatment. The one who knows he does not know becomes the patient, to be doctored by those who profess to know. The supervisor's *aporia* – his sense of what he has and what he lacks – has been misinterpreted by all concerned as a disease.

(2) *Sanctions*

The administration also uses more direct methods than restricting record-writing to dependable groups in order to foster reliability. Most entries in the medical record must be signed, thus making the record-writer responsible for his record.

Requiring a signature would seem to involve an implicit recognition on the part of the administrator that records are only contingently knowledge. If the observer's speech fails to mirror the event, then the record is not knowledge but opinion. As opinion it will belong to someone and it becomes relevant to know to whom it belongs. Hence the need for the signature. Note that with a signature the bureaucrat has a new option at his disposal. If he decides to rely on the observer, he can know about the event. If he does not rely on the observer, then he can at least know whom he finds unreliable. In a sense, he has a record either way – either a record of the event or a record of who made the opinionated speech. Thus there are at least two senses in which Erikson and Gilbertson's point that a record is 'a record of the personnel who contributed to it' may be taken: (1) obviously, personnel may figure in the events reported in adequate records but also (2) by requiring signatures, administrators have the option of treating any record, not as a report about an event, but as a record of who failed to let an event speak. If administrators choose this option then, although they cannot know the event, they can know who they blame for their lack of knowledge, they can know who it is that is unreliable. Given the possibility of this option, we can say that signing a record might serve to encourage observers to be reliable by reminding opinionated record-writers who are tempted to contaminate the record that they may not succeed in getting others to accept their version of the event. Since they are known (by signing), if it is decided that they are unreliable, then what may become 'known' is not their version of the event but the fact that they are unreliable.[21]

Obviously, the writer becomes legally responsible for what he has written by signing his name.[22] However, the signer is also accountable in more subtle ways. His colleagues will often look at an entry which he has signed and then ask him: 'Why did you write *that*?' Similarly, at staff meetings which use medical records, authors of an entry will often be asked to explain what they have written. The fact that record-writers will sometimes refuse to sign documents or think twice before signing offers some evidence of signatures acting as sanctions controlling record-writers' behaviour.[23]

Another aspect of the responsibility of doctors for their entries in the record is the fact that some important entries must be 'authenticated' by superiors. An official Mont Royal Hospital memorandum states that 'all histories, physical exams, and summaries entered in the record by interns and first and second year residents must be authenticated.' Although, in practice, the 'authentication' procedure consists of a careless signature by a busy man, the fact that the initial-writer knows that others may be held responsible for what he writes could foster reliability.[24]

Clearly a signature will not rule out unreliability. Indeed, the fact that records must be signed makes some record-writers even less inclined to be accurate when, as so often, the truth would incriminate them. Requiring a signature will not really help the truth come out, then, because it instils fear where courage is what is necessary. When a very old lady with severe disfiguring bruises was brought into the emergency room by her husband, the nurse said to me: 'I'm sure he beats her.' Yet the nurse's description of the woman's complaint read: 'Husband says she falls a lot.' We blame her sarcasm (dishonesty) on the supervisor. As Socrates realized, there is no good escape from his irony. If we are not permitted and encouraged to say what we think but do not actually know, we will be forced to think we know more than we are saying.

(3) *Replications*

Administrators use the same tactic to foster reliability that social scientists use. They attempt to have two or more observers, working independently, write up the same events. A patient's history is supposed to be taken by three doctors. Two doctors are supposed to give him physicals. Daily 'progress' reports are supposed to be written by both attending and resident physicians.

It is true that doctors have ways of skirting rules about replications. It is never certain that two entries about the same event, when they appear in the record, constitute an authentic replication. Since doctors writing later entries have access to earlier entries, often the second note will merely reproduce the first.[25] However, just the fact that replications are required shows that the administration is attempting to exercise control over record-writers.

In the activity of replication, having two or more observers is not, in fact, a device for increasing individuality, variety, or opinionated speech but for decreasing these extraneous influences. In the peculiar logic of non-participation and self-denial which characterizes observers and record-users, it is hoped that the many will do, so to speak, less than the one. Adding amounts to subtracting since it is intended that the many will have less effect on the event than the one would. How does this logic work? Any actual observer could be opinionated and hence unreliable. If he is opinionated, there is the danger that the speech which belongs to him could be mistaken for the speech which belongs to the event. The idea of replication tries to manage this danger by increasing the number of observers and being interested only in what they have in common. Since the more people, the less they will have in common, it is hoped that with enough people what they will continue to have in common is what would be there if they had nothing in common, the impact of that which affects them in spite of rather than because of themselves, i.e., the pristine event which is supposed to speak through them rather than because of them.

Although Galtung writes that we replicate to eliminate 'observations that belong to one particular person . . . and cannot be shared by others',[26] more rigorously, it is not what observers share that replication is after. Increasing the number of observers is intended to bring observers to the point where they will share nothing, and hence the event will be available as what they still have in common in spite of their complete differentness. What they will have in common under these circumstances is not really shared by them since it is not their joint possession. Rather, since ideally they share nothing, if their speech continues to show something common to them, it must not be their speech (opinion) which is being expressed; it must be the world's speech.

Inevitably, there will be times when record-writers supposedly observing the same event will have to face the fact that they have different opinions:

> Patient is having only minimal signs of withdrawal if at all. It is my feeling that if surgeon feels very strongly about treating with narcotics temporarily (or with methadone) then child should be transferred to surgical floor.

An intern writes:

> Cannot understand note of 6/4 by surgeons. In the presence of palpable node, [unreadable] will be found in scaline biopsy in virtually 100% of the cases.

Two notes for the same patient on the same day by different doctors read:

> 4/28 Feeling much better today. No chest pains.
>
> Burns
>
> 4/28 This is a very sick lady . . . I feel that the patient is in coronary heart failure . . . I feel, too, that a more positive approach to the problem is in order.
>
> Beck

Later they write:

> 5/16 Doing well. Patient ready for discharge. Would think this is more advisable than sending to Rehabilitation in view of fact her home would be more conducive to her emotional state. Will discuss with attending physician [i.e. Dr Beck].
>
> Burns
>
> 5/17 Patient has many anxieties. She lives alone and is fearful of 'heart attack' at night. Intensive separation from sheltered medical environment such as Rehabilitation offers is, in my opinion, ideal. Of course I *do not* advise prolonged stay at Rehabilitation.
>
> Beck
>
> 5/27 Patient is ready for discharge but now complains no one to take care of her at home. Patient insists on going to

Rehabilitation. This presents a problem to house staff.
Active decision by Dr Beck needed.

Burns

5/28 It has been the desire of this observer to discharge the
patient at the earliest possible moment. Transfer to
Rehabilitation was denied. In the meantime patient has
developed what appears to be an asthmatic [unreadable].
The plan is to discharge at the earliest possible moment.

Beck

Still later Beck is complaining:

6/2 Wheezing again, this time following no specific drugs.
Has had recurrent shoulder pain yesterday. Patient has
made no progress. Interference with her transfer to
Rehabilitation appears to be detrimental to her recovery.

Beck

All these disagreements are much more like arguments than
they are like productive conversations. Pro- and anti-
methadone factions talk past each other rather than discuss the
worth of their respective treatments. The intern is more willing
to be unable to understand the surgeon than to try. And in the
long 'dialogue' between Burns and Beck, the differing commitments to bed and patient which make them disagree are
never aired and hence cannot be resolved. Instead of the
thoughtful resolution of problems, we have all the strong feel-
ings, lack of understanding, claims and counter-claims,
resentments, and insistence that the supervisor wanted to
avoid. By this point in our discussion, though, the acrimony
should not surprise. By expecting everyone to know rather
than to think, i.e., to agree unthinkingly, the supervisor produces people who, whenever they think, i.e., realize they are
not mere replicas of one another, will fail to agree.

(4) *Linking bureaucratic and professional tasks*

A key administrative strategy for producing dependable observers is to make the record-writer's medical and bureaucratic
tasks coincide so that the same record is meant to serve both
bureaucratic and professional users. An example will clarify

this point. A pathologist does not perform two separate activities in reporting his findings to the attending physician and producing a record for the files. Using carbon paper he engages in both activities at once. A pathologist who wanted to hide the fact that a patient's tumour was benign from the medical record will also have to hide this fact from the surgeon waiting to cut. Similarly, if the pathologist wanted to present his colleagues with only an elliptical version of the event, he would have to present that to bureaucratic users too.

Having two or more records produced at once is a nice device for minimizing observer participation. If the two records were produced by two separate acts, the observer would, of course, have twice as many chances to intervene by imposing his own desire on the event. In addition, the fact that the same record is used by both doctors and bureaucrats has some additional significance which makes it compatible with what has just been said about replication. Instead of the number of observers, now the size of the audience is being increased. Those concerned with reliability may be hoping that with more than one audience (bureaucrats as well as doctors) the observer will not have available the interactionally useful device of tailoring the message to the audience. More than one audience is going to hear the same message. If the audiences have nothing in common (nothing they all want to hear) the observer may have nothing he wants to tell them all. If he has nothing he wants to say, perhaps he will allow the event to speak more clearly through him.

Instead of permitting the difference in type of audience to generate the difference between the *Phaedo* and the *Apology*, the supervisor would have tried to make Socrates 'consistent' by forcing him to speak at the same time to his friends and enemies. And there seems to be some support for the supervisor's impulse because from the *Apology* we might think that Socrates is merely willing to accept death in the same way that he accepts life whereas from the *Phaedo* we learn that, being a philosopher, he always wanted to die. He lets his enemies learn that they have not managed to do him any harm but not that they have actually done him a favour. Yet this is no simple case of inconsistency since, while what he tells Phaedo *et al.* is not for Meletus and the other accusers to hear, what he tells

Meletus could be for Phaedo as well. Instead of saying contradictory things to different audiences, he speaks more freely to those who are his friends. Friends have no need of the carbon paper since we tell them the truth anyway. Supervising now looks not like controlling, guiding, or watching over us but seeking to overhear us. However, the spy's problems are legion of course. If his enemies know he is there they will stop talking freely. Hence, the fact, already partly documented under other headings, that all records about topics which are touchy from a supervisory viewpoint are defensive. It is always patients who die, never doctors who kill them. 'Proper' procedures, even those that self-respecting doctors would never stoop to perform, are always reported to have been followed. When addicts escape, it is never the doctor's but the addict's fault. When patients 'refuse' treatment, the onus does not fall on the doctor for failing to convince them.

On the other hand, if the spy does manage to hide himself, first of all he will have to suffer under what, from his perspective, is mostly dross. All the records seem much too long to supervisors, as indicated by the fact that supervisors require 'discharge summaries'. Details which, at the very least, it is hard to imagine one who is supposed to be taking the larger perspective using, abound:

> Called nurse to use bedpan. 'I had a laxative today – so I'm going to try to move my bowels.' Had fair sized bowel movement. 'I hope I didn't mess up the bed. I know it's so messy for you girls to clean up. I don't like to bother anyone.' Daughter, who is a nun, visits this afternoon. Refused all supper.

> Thank you for the consultation.

> I will be out of town Friday, Saturday, Sunday. Call Dr Zyw in emergency.

The supervisor's practical solution to the problem of detail, requiring summaries, has its own problems to be discussed later. Most important, if Meletus had overheard what Socrates told his friends the information would have done him no good since what he needs to know is not that he did Socrates a favour but that he failed to do him any harm. The spy-supervisor is another instance of our basic point: if we try to learn more than is good for us, i.e., to know rather than to think, i.e., overhear rather than learn by asking, all that happens is that we fail to get any good out of what we can learn. Instead of gaining knowledge by spying, the supervisor is just showing yet again his reluctance to earn loyalty through ruling, thereby losing his potential friends.

In discussing four administrative tactics for fostering dependability, our point has been to show that these tactics do not 'work' if by that is meant remedy the underlying problem. The underlying 'problem' – the fact that humans think rather than know – resurfaces with irremediable regularity in its various frustrating guises, one of which is the very formulation of those who could rule as supervisors.

5 Completeness

In the previous chapter, we treated administrative tactics fostering reliability as a methodic response to the bureaucrat's dilemma that, although the truth of records cannot be directly determined because the bureaucrat is not present at the event, the bureaucrat as user must nevertheless satisfy himself that speech does not participate in his use of the record. Another methodic solution to the same dilemma is to reorganize the idea of presence to the local event by extending what is meant by the event to include the record. Administrators can gain presence and hence make possible their non-participation by reconceiving of the record as itself the event. If the record itself can be conceived of as the event, then the administrator, who obviously can be present with the record, is no longer necessarily in a state of ignorance. The problem generated by the administrator's absence at the original event can be overcome, then, not just by surrogate presence as was the case with reliability, but also by making the record itself into a thing which, like the observer's original events, shows itself as what it is and so can be assessed, read, and used, without reference to the original event. If the event can, as it were, be extended to the administrator, then the administrator, like the observer, need not express his opinions or otherwise intrude and the event (now the record) can be protected.

It remains true, of course, that whether a record mirrors an event cannot be determined by those who are absent when the event occurs. However, records can be assessed in terms of standards other than their effectiveness in mirroring events. For example, records can be evaluated according to whether they possess various bureaucratically necessary forms and whether the forms have been 'completed', i.e., whether all questions on the form have been answered and whether all the

102

forms have been signed. Such evaluation amounts to redefin-
ing the record as a visible event at which the bureaucrat, being
present, can sustain a selfless and neutral stance that does not
corrupt the pristine certainty of the event (now the record).
Thus bureaucratic standards are themselves a method for controlling the (one who makes the) construction of the record so
that the selfsame principle of non-participation which record-
writers were asked to follow can also be followed by record-
users. One may indeed marvel that the idea by which a record
is made synonymous with the event it originally recorded – the
idea that the event shall show itself as what it is – is now
turned around and made into the criterion of adequate records.
An adequate record becomes not one which actually mirrors
the event (since knowledge of the accuracy of the record is not
available to those who are absent) but one which shows itself
to be adequate by appearing to be adequate to any bureaucrat
who looks at it.

Thus, while it may be that standards like bureaucratically
defined completeness seem *ad hoc* in that they are far removed
from the obvious original purpose of making a record, they
remain in accord with the grounds of the activity of recording.
This is to say that for bureaucracy, so-called *ad hoc* standards
can sustain an interest in the truth of records whereas at first
blush it would seem that the bureaucrat's absence at the
appearance of the original event precludes any such assessment. It is the conspicuous task of the bureaucrat to re-achieve
the original aim of the activity of recording, which is to obtain
knowledge rather than to create opinion, by letting events
speak, even in the face of his absence at the original event. It is
the bureaucrat's task to remember that adequate knowledge is
obtainable only by refusing to speak so as to let events speak to
him. He fulfils his task by treating records as things which
show themselves to be what they are, thereby rendering
further speech unnecessary. The familiar, general notion that
bureaucratic organization leads to the displacement of senti-
ments from *goals* (in this case obtaining truthful records) to
means (in this case evaluating records)[1] does not really capture
this phenomenon, since the displacement (if such it be)
remains in accord with the original grounds of the activity of
observation.

The hospital administration's overriding interest is in the *completeness* of records. We shall show how the concern with completeness and the way in which completeness is defined, while seemingly contradicting the goals of record-keeping, in fact manage to re-achieve, within the bureaucratic context, the same basic record-keeper's principles which we have been analyzing throughout. A major theme of the discussion, then, is that evaluation of records in terms of completeness is compatible with the basic principle that records are supposed to report the truth, the truth being defined as an observer defines it, namely as that which presents itself by itself without any need for co-participation with it by speakers. Just as those who are present at the event become observers by letting the event present itself to them, those who wish to evaluate become readers (and readers for whom reading amounts, analytically, to observation), by letting the record's completeness present itself to them. The reader is able to achieve exactly the same kind of passivity which the observer was able to achieve by treating the record the way the observer treated the event – as a thing which is showing him what it is. Difficulties over completeness will then amount to a further instance of the difficulty that is seeking to avoid one's human, opinionated fate. The supervisor is like Crito, wanting Socrates to 'complete' his life so that Crito need have no part in his death. The trouble is that the situation is such, the situation is *always* such, that Crito can avoid a part in Socrates' death only by having a part in his life. If records are to be 'completed', then supervisors, like Crito, will have to explain why. The trouble with the explanations is that *they* are incomplete. Instead of convincing Socrates or record-writers to complete, they may remind them why they chose to end. Here, once again, the supervisor could learn his limits or he could become frustrated. Crito comes to learn that really he was asking Socrates to act without thinking, thereby not completing but contradicting his whole life. Socrates has not completed his life, whatever that means, but he has finished it, i.e., produced an end consistent with what he has been doing all along. If the supervisor could see through his frustration at the perennial incompleteness of records, he could learn that when people do not complete things it is because they think they have already done their part.

1

It is easily noticeable that completeness is the major standard in terms of which records are actually assessed by bureaucrats. Inaccuracy is never directly mentioned in the administration's memoranda about records but incompleteness often is. One memorandum deals exclusively with penalties for incomplete records. The memorandum states that 'failure to fulfil this requirement [completing the record] will automatically author- ize the director's office to suspend admitting privileges and/or to suspend operating privileges.'[2]

Whenever a new kind of information is required for the med- ical record, the memorandum which announces the new requirement includes statements like:[3]

> The completion of . . . [the new form] will be a requisite for a completed chart. If Medical Record, in reviewing charts of discharged patients, finds that this form has not been completed, it will indicate that the chart is an incomplete one and the appropriate disciplinary action will be taken with reference to incomplete records.

Another memorandum notes that 'an unsigned form renders the chart incomplete and will not be accepted by the Medical Record Department.'[4] A manual for hospital administrators also emphasizes, not that records should be truthful, but that they should be complete:[5]

> In all cases the record should be complete to the extent that it presents a comprehensive picture of the patient's illness, together with the physical findings and special reports, such as x-ray and laboratory. Such a record substantiates the diagnosis, warrants the treatment and justifies the end result.

It is not just memoranda and manuals which indicate the administration's overriding interest in the completeness of records. It is also the administration's actions. Three clerks in the Medical Record Room of Mont Royal Hospital constantly attempt to force doctors to finish their records. Indeed, the major reason for which doctors come to the record room is not to study old charts but to finish records. The record room receptionist assumes that a doctor has come to complete records whenever he enters the record room. Thus, she always greets a doctor with: 'You are Dr ———?' or, if she knows him, 'Hello, Dr Hitchcock.' Then, without any indication from the doctor as to the purpose of his visit, she will send a file clerk to find the doctor's incomplete charts.

An entire wall of shelves is used to store incomplete charts. The fact that there are regular procedures for processing incomplete charts and even regular places to store them suggests, of course, that, to the administration, incompleteness is both noticeable and worth correcting. If we understand that bureaucrats remain interested in truth but recognize their status as non-observers of the original event, we can understand completeness as their way of achieving presence, as their way to deny participation, as their way to the real. A clerk or an administrator, sitting in the record room, can decide (using observers' principles) whether a record is bureaucratically complete but not whether it is accurate. Incompleteness (a missing signature, a missing discharge summary) can be easily spotted even by medically naive clerks. These are things which can be seen because they appear just like the observer's original events. The clerks are doing the same basic activity that observers are doing. They are letting what is present speak to them and so guide their speech for them. Thus a concern with completeness does not contradict a concern with truth if by truth is meant commitment to observational principles. The complete record is the observer-bureaucrat's version of the true record in that, as far as he can determine by looking, it shows itself to be true.

Indeed, if bureaucrats did concern themselves with the truth of the record as a mirror of the original event, *then* they would be contradicting observers' principles. They would be trying to gain knowledge without being present. They would be participating. They would be speaking their own minds rather than minding the event. That a record corresponds to an event is the business of those who are there. This the bureaucrat believes, and, far from contradicting this belief, he reasserts it by restricting himself to assessing records as events, rather than the events the records purport to record. Focusing on the completeness of the record transforms the record into the bureaucrat's event and transforms the bureaucrat into an observer who need not participate. We find in chapter 5 as we found in chapter 4 that whereas the bureaucrat and the record-writer may *do* different things (the record-writer looks at events, the bureaucrat looks at records), what they do is different only in the most superficial sense. The different things they are doing amount to the same thing in the sense that they are different expressions (because of differing structural locations) of the same commitment to treating the real as that which will appear to those who would only look for it.

2

We are far from suggesting that the interests of administrators and record-writers never clash. What we are suggesting is that the clash, when it occurs, cannot be understood as a conflict between one goal and another or between a commitment to goals and a commitment to means. Rather, the clash amounts to the fact that the same goal, even the same intention, will result in different behaviour because of different structural locations within the same basic system. The clash is a clash between two parts, each of whom is unwilling to engage in the dialogue (the recognition of incompleteness) which would allow them to fit into a whole. An example will help concretize the discussion.

Although administrators take the task of finishing records very seriously, doctors are not so committed to this principle. The administration's attempts to get records completed amount to a perennial concern: clerks are constantly trying to force record-writers to finish, and yet record-writers persist in not finishing. Doctors take a lighthearted attitude toward the threats of record room clerks. One doctor said, 'They're sending me threatening letters; I'm gonna report them to the FBI.' A doctor yelled to his colleague as the latter was entering the record room: 'Welcome to the Black Hole of Calcutta.' A serious-minded doctor was just as uncommitted to the task of finishing his records. He commented: 'This is such an unrewarding way to spend time.'

Once they are in the record room, one of the major jobs for doctors trying to finish their records is the dictation of discharge summaries. Usually, doctors performing this task show distance from what they are doing. Almost uniformly, doctors adopt a bored, steady monotone while doing the dictation. One day, amidst general laughter, a doctor unplugged his colleague's tape recorder while the colleague was dictating. Doctors do not consider finishing records to be a very important, demanding, or even necessary task. Thus, when the emergency room receptionist asked a doctor to finish his record by signing it, the doctor shouted: 'What the hell for? I've got better things to do.' Indeed, the very fact that charts, unlike, for example, operations, often remain unfinished indicates the relative indifference of doctors to completing their records.

In order to understand these data, we must be quite clear about the sense in which records tend to be unfinished. What is usually seen to be missing by the bureaucrats is either a signature or a discharge summary. Bureaucrats miss these but record-writers do not because of the different ways the two different actors have of doing the same activity. In other words, the doctors' indifference and the bureaucrats' concern are products of a deeper agreement between them that knowledge can be obtained only by denying one's own participation so as to let things show themselves. Doctors' indifference to signing a record or writing a discharge summary is an affirmation rather than a denial of the principles of record-keeping.[6] An adequate record is one in which the self of the record-writer does not intrude on the event. Therefore, the doctor is right to be indifferent to signing because, *qua* record-writer, he knows that who wrote the record is not supposed to matter. The indifference to signing, then, could represent his commitment to self-denial. Indifference to his own name expresses his belief that who he is does not make a difference to the record. Similarly, a discharge summary should also be a matter of indifference since it is (supposed to) add nothing to what has already been said. It is (supposed to) repeat what is already there to be seen anyway. From a record-writer's point of view, a discharge summary does not finish a record at all since a record is finished when the events it reports cease to appear and hence cease to need mirroring. To an observer, a discharge summary is an appendage to an already finished record. Delays in doing discharge summaries are much more common than outright refusals to do them. These delays are also understandable in terms of the record-writer's principles. Unlike the original event, the record which is supposed to mirror it is, at least ideally, permanent. Therefore the discharge summary, which will be a record of the record, can be done at any time. There is no rush since the event it will mirror (the record) will not go away.

The bureaucrat will not accept the record-writer's logic here, of course, but the important point for us to see is the basis of the disagreement. It is obviously elliptical to say, as hospital bureaucrats do, that record-writers do not finish records. Record-writers do finish *their own* records but they do not finish the bureaucrat's records. The bureaucrat's records will be finished, not when the record completely mirrors the event, but when the record appears to be complete according to bureaucratic standards. By *not* completing this record, the record-writer is asserting his claim to have said only what the event permits him to say. By demanding this record's completion, the bureaucrat is expressing his desire to be able to make the same claim. The disagreement is the product of a deeper agreement, an agreement that speech can contaminate events and that the solution is to let events or appearances do the speaking.

Both the record-writer's and supervisor's desires for completeness flounder on the existence of each other since *qua* others they will have different notions of what is enough. The threats, the delaying tactics, the indifference, the jokes, and the shouts, then, are all ways of refusing to admit that their respective parts are not the whole, and therefore could agree with each other. So it is really *lack* of speech which contaminates their relationship in the sense that they clash because their supposed completeness makes both unwilling to hear what the other wants and why. If Crito had had his way there would have been no dialogue about his plan for Socrates' escape because 'the time for deliberation is over, and there is only one thing to be done, which must be done this very night, and if we delay at all will be no longer practicable or possible.'[7] Socrates says, 'Dear Crito, your zeal is invaluable, if a right one; but if wrong, the greater the zeal the greater the danger, and therefore we ought to consider whether I shall or shall not do as you say.'[8] The irony here is that really it is Crito who wants to escape, i.e., from thinking, and Socrates who thwarts the plan, by insisting that they think about it. Crito has panicked so he needs to be reminded that there is no escape from thinking since, even if he convinced Socrates to escape, he would have to live with that and so would Socrates. Record-writer and supervisor are both trying not to live with what they have to do (their need for thought, their incompleteness) by getting the other to do it for them. At the end of the dialogue, though Crito does not get Socrates to escape, he does get him to say: 'Be assured, then, that anything more which you may say to shake my faith will be said in vain. Yet speak, if you have anything to say.'[9] Crito can respond: 'I have nothing to say.'[10] There is a kind of agreement here which record-writer and supervisor, though they are nowhere near as different as Socrates and Crito, fail to achieve. Both are not escaping from their responsibility, Socrates by staying in Athens, Crito by doing his best to convince Socrates to escape. Unlike the supervisor and record-writer, Crito learns how to be finished without being complete.

The supervisor could begin to take responsibility by admitting why he is so eager to have the item that is especially relevant to the bureaucrat's completed record, namely the presence of a doctor's or nurse's signature after every entry. Why is the presence of the signature so important? By getting the writer to sign the record the administration has gotten the writer to declare or say (by signing) that the record is adequate. The declaration is then treated by the bureaucrat as that which is showing itself to him. He does not know whether the record mirrors the event but he does know that someone *says* that the record mirrors the event. That someone has said that the record is adequate becomes the fact (event) which is presenting itself to the administrator. The administration can therefore point to the declaration as its reason for saying what it says about the record or, better, as its reason for not having to say anything about the record. If a record is signed, instead of having to decide (speak) about its adequacy, the bureaucrat takes the fact that the record-writer says it is adequate as deciding things for him. The record appears to be adequate in that the writer has declared it to be adequate. By claiming that his record is adequate, the writer is making his record appear to be adequate and is therefore making it possible for potential readers to treat his record as a thing which is showing them what it is, as a thing which they can observe, as a thing with which they can act precisely as the original observer is supposed to act with the original event.

Unlike the original record-writer's speech, the correctness of the signature need not be determined by matching it against some thing external to itself. The signature's adequacy is not contingent on whether it mirrors the world. Strictly speaking, the signature is not a description of another event but itself the event. The bureaucracy needs to be able to treat speech, not as opinionated and therefore uncertain, but as knowledgeable and definite. It does this by insisting on a kind of speech (the signature) which becomes adequate not by being right but merely by being done. Merely by signing, the signer is doing something. He is saying he is responsible. By saying that he is responsible, he is removing the bureaucracy from responsibility for its speech. The bureaucracy need not check his record against the original (now absent) event. The signer is making it possible for the investigation (of speech) to stop by making a speech which says, claims, shows, and legally establishes where the responsibility lies.

When it is remembered that a signature is not a speech about some other thing but itself an observable thing, it becomes unsurprising to note that whether the 'correct' person signs a record is irrelevant to record room clerks. It is easy to document that the clerks do not care who signs the chart. In the record room, it is more important that someone signs a chart, so that it can be considered complete, than that the person who actually wrote the record sign it. A clerk faced with the common problem of a doctor who had left the hospital permanently without signing some of his charts approached a doctor who happened to be in the record room, with the relevant chart and the following statement: 'He's not here any more so you're gonna have to sign it; sorry about that.' Clerks often run up to doctors and ask them to sign charts they have not even read, much less written. The record room clerk's indifference to who signs the record does not conflict with the basic idea of requiring a signature. He who signs *takes* responsibility by making himself appear to be the producer of the record. The signature affirms responsibility by making the signer claim to be and therefore (according to the viewpoint of reader-observers who are supposed to be passive) *be* the author. Bureaucrats are indifferent to who signs since the signer, merely by signing, will appear to be the writer and so, from the perspective of those who need not decide about speech since they treat speech (signatures) as things which exist and are adequate merely because they have been done, will be the writer.

Again, a Mertonian analysis would have failed to adequately describe the phenomenon we are studying. We might have thought, if we had followed Merton's principles, that bureaucrats were failing to see the intent behind the rule by accepting any signature rather than the 'correct' one and we might therefore have been content to describe our bureaucrats as ritualists. However, it has turned out that the very rule that a signature should be obtained, and not the fortuitous ritualism of some of the rule followers makes possible and rational the clerk's behaviour in accepting any signature. It is not that clerks who accept any signature fail to see the intent behind the rule but that the rule we are studying implicitly asks clerks to ignore the question of intent. The Mertonian approach fails to understand that the idea behind some rules, in this case the rule requiring a signature, is to overcome the constellation of problems implicit in the concept of 'intent'. To think about speech in terms of its intent is to make speech indefinite all over again. It is to make any speech problematic by asking us to ask the speech: 'What does it really mean?' The point of the signature is to rid speech of this problem of intent or meaning by getting someone to *declare* his intent, in this case his intent to have spoken the truth. The declaration is supposed to solve the problem of intent by making intent into something that can be spoken rather than that which any speech leaves unsaid.

To query the signature (as Merton might expect a non-ritualistic clerk to do) amounts to querying the speech and so acknowledging exactly what the bureaucracy does not want to acknowledge, namely that the signature is not an event but a speech and so raises a problem (its intent) by solving a problem (the intent of the record). By *not* querying the signature, on the other hand, the clerk is being a good bureaucrat by making speech into a thing which establishes itself (an event) rather than a thing which requires participation. Even if the signature turns out in the end to be a fraud, this is still no problem for the bureaucrat since he can still excuse himself (deny the need for participation) by pointing to the signature's existence. His argument can be: the record may be a fraud, but he was not to know since what was appearing to him (his event) was that someone said (by signing) that the record was true. At the very least, the clerks' behaviour is not a displacement from the original organizational goal, since the original goal implicit in requiring a signature (the goal of ridding speech of its contingent status) is fulfilled rather than displaced by acquiring any rather than a 'correct' signature.

Just as 'knowledge' (the signature) is really the supervisor's excuse, 'ignorance' is really Socrates' reason. The supervisor excuses himself whenever Socrates begins. Just before the discussion which takes him and Glaucon as close to the good as they can get, Socrates, apparently at lowest ebb, admits to Adeimantos that when he speaks of the good he feels 'like a blind man who feels his way along the right road'. He asks whether 'he wishes to behold what is blind and crooked and base (i.e., an opinion) when others will tell you of brightness and beauty.'[11] Adeimantos, realizing that his apparent wish to know the good will not be realized, drops out of the discussion. Yet Socrates still comes to speak his mind, thanks to Glaucon, who breaks in with: 'I must implore you, Socrates, not to turn away just as you are reaching the goal; if you will only give such an explanation of the good as you have already given of justice and temperance and the other virtues, we shall be satisfied.'[12] We presented one version of the humour here back in chapter 3. Now it seems less like a simple joke at Glaucon's expense and more like irony. The one who apparently wants to know rather than think, e.g., Adeimantos with his efforts to get Socrates to say positively what the good is or the supervisor with his pursuit of signatures, does not even have the desire, hence they excuse themselves when confronted with their ignorance. The one whose willingness to only think makes him look and feel ignorant is the one who truly wants to know.

3

In addition to the signature, other aspects of the record in which the bureaucracy maintains an interest demonstrate how the bureaucracy, by pursuing its goal of letting things speak to it so as to make participation unnecessary, has converted the record into a thing which can show itself to be what it is.

A clerk in the record room was discussing a dilemma concerning a patient's chart. The patient had died in the emergency room before two essential parts of the record could be completed, the history of the illness and the physical examination. The clerk suggested to the doctor whose responsibility the chart was that he write: 'Patient came in in excellent condition. Deceased fifteen minutes later.' We can make sense out of her joke in terms of the principles we have already discussed. From her point of view, what mattered was to have a record rather than a 'correct' record (in a correspondence sense of correct). What mattered was to get something on paper. Again, we have the record as contingent not on another event, but on itself. The record is adequate when it has those things, e.g., a history of the illness and a physical examination, which records are supposed to have. When it has these things, it will appear to be a record and so can be used by the bureaucracy. The clerk is conceiving of the record as a thing. The clerk wants something on paper so that the record can be observably a record. What she wants is compatible with (1) bureaucratic commitment to the principles of observation and (2) her absence at the original event.

Interesting forms to consider from the point of view of the bureaucratic desire to treat the record as a thing are 'consent' forms. These must be signed by patients or near relatives before certain major procedures like operations and transfusions can be performed. A patient 'consents' by signing a form which reads:

> I, ——, hereby give my voluntary consent to the performance of the following procedure, as indicated, with whatever anesthesia is prescribed upon ——. I certify that the above procedure has been explained to me and I understand the diagnostic or treatment necessary for it. Mont Royal Hospital, its medical staff, and employees are

hereby released from the liability of the results of this procedure.

There are extensive regulations designed to ensure that these forms are signed and entered into the record before patients undergo surgery. However, there are no written regulations requiring that 'consent' forms accurately describe what occurred between patient and doctor.

According to the principles of the activity of observing, consent forms are all wrong. Except for a few blank spaces, these forms are written, not by present observers, but by absent administrators. All of the forms are uniform so they cannot vary with the peculiarities of individual events. As descriptions of events, clearly, consent forms are inadequate.

However, the purpose of consent forms is not to represent events. What is important is not whether a form accurately describes events. Rather, what is important is the mere presence of a signed form in the record. Although a signed form may not be an accurate representation, it is complete in the sense that it says everything that must be said in order to protect the hospital against malpractice suits. That is, the consent form need not be 'accurate' because strictly speaking it is not a description at all. It is not a report of an event. It *is* an event. Merely by being there it shows all concerned that consent has been obtained. It *is* the consent. As such it fulfils rather than negates observers' principles by being understandable as an attempt to solve the problem of the administrator's absence by bringing the consent to him and so making it possible for him to reconstitute himself as an observer present at the event (the record).

No doubt doctors obtain 'consent' by claiming to know what they only think, thereby making possible dissent whenever the opinionated nature of the treatment comes to be disclosed. Socrates is willing to risk the pursuit of dialogue rather than consent. Therefore he need not hide his own uncertainty, lack of understanding, and liability in the treatment. The doctors would worry that Socrates will never get any patients, missing the point that he does not need any because everyone is getting his treatment whether they consent or not. His treatment is his decisive presentation of what he is, which allows and encourages the others, through consent, dissent, and the various other commitments, to come to grips with themselves.

Research note

All the hospital data were gathered between September 1969 and August 1971, when I was a project supervisor at a large public hospital in New York City. As a social scientist actually working for the hospital, I was allowed ready access to all areas of the hospital which I wished to study. Most of my research time was spent in the hospital's medical record room. I identified myself as a researcher interested in medical records and was allowed to examine the files as often and as thoroughly as I liked. I noted down verbatim any parts of the record which seemed to me to be of interest. I was also able to observe the various kinds of interaction that occurred in the record room, since my desk was conveniently located in the same room where all the clerks worked and where doctors came to complete their records.

The other major piece of research I carried out was the observation of the actual process of record-writing in two areas of the hospital: the emergency room and a rehabilitation centre. In both cases, I told persons in charge that I was interested in the record-keeping process and was invited to stand (or sit) at the main desk and observe the ongoing business of the hospital (including the writing of records). In the rehabilitation centre, where the pace was slower, I also participated in a good deal of the routine daily work, attending meetings, accompanying nurses on visits to patients' rooms, etc.

From time to time I conducted both formal and informal interviews with doctors, nurses, and administrators in order to elicit their opinions about issues and problems involved in record-keeping. In addition, the administration allowed me to study an extensive collection of memoranda concerning records and related topics.

Notes

1 Introduction

1 R. G. Collingwood, *The Idea of History*, Oxford: Clarendon Press, 1946, pp. 9–10.
2 G. Kitson Clark, *The Critical Historian*, London: Heinemann, 1967, p. 76.
3 Louis Gottschalk, Clyde Kluckhohn, and Robert Angell, *The Use of Personal Documents in History, Anthropology and Sociology*, bulletin no. 53, New York: Social Science Research Council, 1945, p. 8.
4 Ibid., p. 35.
5 London: Routledge & Kegan Paul, 1952.
6 2 vols, University of Chicago Press, 1918.
7 T. J. Roethlisberger and William Dickson, *Management and the Worker*, Harvard University Press, 1939, p. 27.
8 G. P. Lodge, 'Pilot Stature in Relation to Cockpit Size: A Hidden Factor in Navy Jet Air Craft Accidents', *American Psychologist*, 17, 1963, p. 468.
9 H. Hyman and Daniel Katz, 'Morale in War Industries', in T. Newcomb and E. Hartley (eds), *Readings in Social Psychology*, New York: Holt, 1947, pp. 437–47.
10 Alan Kerckhoff, Curt Back and Norman Miller, 'Socio-Metric Patterns in Hysterical Contagion', *Sociometry*, 28 (1), March 1965, pp. 2–16.
11 Walter D. Connor, 'Juvenile Delinquency in the USSR: Some Quantitative and Qualitative Indicators', *American Sociological Review*, 35 (2), April 1970, pp. 283–97. For summaries of studies which have used written records see Eugene J. Webb *et al.*, *Unobtrusive Measures*, Chicago: Rand McNally, 1966, pp. 53–111.
12 Matilda White Riley, *Sociological Research, I, A Case Approach*, New York: Harcourt, Brace & World, 1963, p. 243.
13 Claire Selltiz *et al.*, *Research Methods in Social Relations*, London: Methuen, 1965, p. 316.
14 Aaron V. Cicourel, *Method and Measurement in Sociology*, Chicago: Free Press, 1964, p. 143.

15 Jack Douglas, *The Social Meanings of Suicide*, Princeton University Press, 1968, p. 191.
16 Gideon Sjoberg and Roger Nett, *A Methodology for Social Research*, New York: Harper & Row, 1968, p. 163.
17 Ibid., p. 164.
18 Thomas Cochran *et al.*, *The Social Sciences in Historical Study*, New York: Social Science Research Council, 1954, pp. 160–1.
19 William Goode, 'The Theory and Measurement of Family Change', in Eleanor Sheldon and Wilbert Moore (eds), *Indicators of Social Change*, New York: Russell Sage Foundation, 1968, p. 312.
20 Gottschalk *et al.*, op. cit., p. 8.
21 Goode, op. cit., p. 314.
22 Harold Garfinkel, *Studies in Ethnomethodology*, Englewood Cliffs, N.J.: Prentice-Hall, 1967, p. 191.
23 Jesse Houwk Shera, *Historians, Books and Libraries*, Western Reserve University Press, 1953, p. 17.
24 Gottschalk *et al.*, op. cit., p. 16.
25 Ibid., p. 22.
26 Ibid., p. 41.
27 See especially chapter 4 below.
28 See chapter 2.
29 See chapter 3.
30 See chapters 2 and 4.
31 See chapters 2 and 5.
32 Shera, op cit., p. 17.
33 Melville Dalton, 'Preconceptions and Methods in Men Who Manage', in Phillip Hammond (ed.), *Sociologists At Work*, New York: Basic Books, 1964, p. 74.
34 Alan Blum and Peter McHugh, 'The Social Ascription of Motives', *American Sociological Review*, 36, February 1971, pp. 98–9, footnote.
35 Garfinkel, op. cit., pp. 186–207.
36 Ibid., p. 195.

2 Observations and records

1 'Observation' is being used in a broad sense which we specify at some length below.
2 Claire Selltiz *et al.*, *Research Methods in Social Relations*, London: Methuen, 1965, p. 200.
3 Louis Gottschalk, Clyde Kluckhohn and Robert Angell, *The Use of Personal Documents in History, Anthropology and Sociology*, bulletin no. 53, New York: Social Science Research Council, 1945, p. 42.
4 Melville Dalton, 'Preconceptions and Methods in Men Who

Manage', in Phillip Hammond (ed.), *Sociologists At Work*, New
York: Basic Books, 1964, p. 74. See also Blanche Geer, 'First Days
in the Field', in ibid., p. 326.
5 Carl Weick, 'Systematic Observational Methods', in Gardner
Lindzey and Elliot Aronson (eds), *The Handbook of Social Psychology*,
Reading, Mass.: Addison-Wesley, 1968, vol. 2, p. 369.
6 Nathaniel Hawthorne, *The Blithedale Romance*, complete works,
London: Kegan Paul, n.d., vol. 5.
7 Weick, op. cit., p. 373. See also Eugene J. Webb *et al.*, *Unobtrusive
Measures*, Chicago: Rand McNally, 1966.
8 In the following anecdote told by Whyte, Doc can be seen as
making the same point. *He* can know what happened because he
was present while Whyte cannot know because he was absent:
'[The] full awareness of the nature of my study stimulated Doc to
look for and point out to me the sorts of observations that I was
interested in. Often when I picked him up at the flat where he
lived with his sister and brother-in-law he said to me "Bill, you
should have been around last night. You would have been
interested in this." And then he would go on to tell me what had
happened.' William F. Whyte, *Street Corner Society*, University of
Chicago Press, 1955, p. 301.
9 On the growth of record-keeping systems, see Stanton Wheeler,
'Problems and Issues in Record-Keeping', in Wheeler (ed.), *On
Record*, New York: Russell Sage Foundation, 1970, pp. 10–11.
10 Weber has made the classic statement of this position. See H. H.
Gerth and C. W. Mills (eds), *From Max Weber*, London: Routledge
& Kegan Paul, 1948, p. 197. See also Peter Blau, *The Dynamics of
Bureaucracy*, University of Chicago Press, 1963, pp. 36–55.
11 Abraham Kaplan, *The Conduct of Inquiry*, San Francisco: Chandler,
1964, p. 127.
12 We shall begin this section with a very brief review of ideas which
have given rise to the version of time corresponding to the
development of observation. It is certainly not our intention to do
this exhaustively, nor to consider alternatives.
13 Matilda White Riley, *Sociological Research, 1, A Case Approach*, New
York: Harcourt, Brace & World, 1963, p. 187.
14 There is an awkwardness in the formulation here due to the fact
that the analysis is incomplete. As will be explained in section 4 of
this chapter, the observer can, in a sense, know the past. He can
know the past if he was present when it was the present.
15 To say that we are 'grounding' the role of the observer is to say that
we are using the method described in chapter 1: we are explicating
the underlying ideas which make the observer possible.
16 Johan Huizinga, 'A Definition of the Concept of History', in

Raymond Klibansky and H. H. Paton (eds), *Philosophy and History*, Essays presented to Ernst Cassirer, Oxford: Clarendon Press, 1936, p. 5.

17 Hence record-writers in the hospital studied tend to write less about patients when their conditions are 'stable'. See chapter 3.

18 For the classic statement see René Descartes, *A Discourse on Method*, trans. by John Veitch, London: Dent, 1912, especially pp. 26–32. Descartes is an interesting example of a man who believes he can know without observing.

19 Observers can also know places to which they *have been*. See section 4.

20 Observers who believe in 'sampling' can be seen as limiting their commitment to observation precisely by arguing that some other places can be understood without one's having been there.

21 We say partially because some of the points made in the next chapter serve to further deepen the analysis.

22 Selltiz *et al.*, op. cit., p. 210.

23 Ibid.

24 A. V. Cicourel, *Methods and Measurement in Sociology*, Chicago: Free Press, 1964, p. 45. See also Hortense Powdermaker, *Hollywood, The Dream Factory*, London: Secker & Warburg, 1951, pp. 5 and 6.

25 Julian Simon, *Basic Research Methods in Social Science*, New York: Random House, 1969, p. 88. See also Arthur J. Vidich, 'Participant Observation and the Collection and Interpretation of Data', *American Journal of Sociology*, 60, January 1955, p. 360. For an argument in favour of non-human recorders, see Joseph Jaffe and Stanley Feldstein, *Rhythms of Dialogue*, New York: Academic Press, 1970, especially p. 3.

26 For a good summary of physiological literature on memory, see Roy E. John, *Mechanisms of Memory*, New York: Academic Press, 1967.

27 Wheeler, op. cit. p. 5.

28 Weick, op. cit., p. 411.

29 This is perhaps the deep ground of those who would characterize bureaucracy as depersonalized. In so far as bureaucracy is a record-keeping organization, the record will have to be kept clear of contamination, given that bureaucracy is among the most pointed modern cases of organizations abiding by the distinction between knowledge and opinion.

30 The relationship between bureaucracy and record-keeping is discussed in more detail in chapters 4 and 5.

31 See n. 14.

32 See Martin Heidegger, *An Introduction to Metaphysics*, New York: Anchor Books, 1961, p. 172.

33 And the future if they will be present when it becomes the present.

3 Records and events

1 Carl Weick, 'Systematic Observational Methods', in Gardner Lindzey and Elliot Aronson (eds), *The Handbook of Social Psychology*, Reading, Mass.: Addison-Wesley, 1968, vol. 2, p. 408.
2 Alfred Schutz, *Collected Papers*, 1968, vol. 2, p. 408. The Hague: Martinus Nijhoff, 1964, vol. 2, p. 61.
3 *What is History?*, London: Macmillan, 1961, p. 6. For a view closer to my own, see R. G. Collingwood, *The Idea of History*, Oxford: Clarendon Press, 1946, especially pp. 20–1, where he briefly makes the argument that history presupposes a particular version of the nature of things.
4 Frederick J. Teggart, *Theory and Processes of History*, University of California Press, 1960, p. 11.
5 A. V. Cicourel, *The Social Organization of Juvenile Justice*, New York: Wiley, 1968, p. 6.
6 See, for example, Ernest Nagel, 'The Logic of Historical Analysis', in Hans Meyerhoff (ed.), *The Philosophy of History in Our Time*, New York: Anchor Books, 1959, p. 207. Two interesting linguistic analyses of narratives also rest on a distinction between the report of the event and the event. See Harvey Sacks, 'On the Analyzability of Stories by Children', in John Gumperz and Dell Hymes (eds), *Directions in Sociolinguistics*, New York: Holt, Rinehart & Winston, 1972, especially p. 330. William Labov and Joshua Waletsky, 'Narrative Analysis; Oral Versions of Personal Experience', in *Essays on the Verbal and Visual Arts*, Proceedings of the 1966 Spring Meeting, American Ethnological Society, University of Washington Press. Our approach to the record-event relationship is differentiated from Labov's below.
7 *The Dialogues of Plato*, trans. by B. Jowett, vol. 2, Oxford: Clarendon Press, 1953, p. 164.
8 Collingwood, op. cit., p. 20.
9 S. Alexander, 'The Historicity of Things', in Raymond Klibansky and H. H. Paton (eds), *Philosophy and History*, Essays presented to Ernst Cassirer, Oxford: Clarendon Press, 1936, p. 11.
10 Martin Heidegger, *An Introduction to Metaphysics*, New York: Anchor Books, 1961, p. 540.
11 Ibid. The idea that, for observers, places belong to things, is not unfamiliar to sociologists. The notion that observation occurs in a 'setting' is the same idea. See Weick, op. cit., pp. 366–9.
12 Stephen Richardson *et al.*, *Interviewing*, London: Basic Books, 1965, p. 9.
13 William Goode, *Explorations in Social Theory*, New York: Oxford University Press, 1973, p. 10.
14 The view that observers are limited to physical things is expressed

121

as follows by Gideon Sjoberg and Roger Nett: 'just what do social scientists observe? They observe physical behaviour, such as walking, waving of arms, facial expressions, and patterned sounds, and the results of physical behaviour, such as writing or tools' (*A Methodology for Social Research*, New York: Harper & Row, 1968, p. 33). See also pp. 160–1.

15 Labov and Waletsky, op. cit., p. 20.

16 Ibid., p. 21.

17 *The Physical Dimensions of Consciousness*, New York: Century, 1933, p. 194.

18 Magdalen Vernon, 'Perception, Attention, and Consciousness', in Paul Bahan (ed.), *Attention*, Princeton: Van Nostrand, 1966, pp. 38–9.

19 Op. cit., p. 198.

20 A. F. Sanders, *Attention and Performance*, Amsterdam: North-Holland, 1967, p. 3.

21 See Boring, op cit., p. 195.

22 See Ernest Mach, *The Analysis of Sensations*, New York: Dover, 1959, pp. 249–50.

23 See for example Wolfgang Kohler, *Gestalt Psychology*, New York: Liveright, 1947, p. 103.

4 Reliability

1 H. H. Gerth and C. W. Mills (eds), *From Max Weber*, London: Routledge & Kegan Paul, 1948, p. 197.

2 Amitai Etzioni, 'Organizational Control Structure', in James March (ed.), *Handbook of Organizations*, Chicago: Rand McNally, 1965, p. 650.

3 Gerth and Mills, op. cit., p. 197. See also Stanton Wheeler, 'Problems and Issues in Record-Keeping', in Wheeler (ed.), *On Record*, New York: Russell Sage Foundation, 1970, *passim*, and Robert Merton, *Social Theory and Social Structure*, New York: Free Press, 1957, pp. 342–3.

4 Peter Blau, *The Dynamics of Bureaucracy*, University of Chicago Press, 1963, pp. 33–65.

5 Kai Erikson and Daniel Gilbertson, 'Case Records in the Mental Hospital', in Wheeler (ed.), op. cit., p. 399.

6 Merton, op. cit., p. 340.

7 Ibid., p. 341.

8 Peter Blau and W. Richard Scott, *Formal Organizations*, London: Routledge & Kegan Paul, 1963, pp. 140–1.

9 The second solution is discussed in the next chapter.

10 Claire Selltiz *et. al.*, *Research Methods in Social Relations*, London: Methuen, 1965, p. 148.

11 Charles Cannel and Robert Kahn, 'Interviewing', in Gardner Lindzey and Elliot Aronson (eds), *The Handbook of Social Psychology*, Reading, Mass.: Addison-Wesley, 1968, vol. 2, p. 359.

12 Carl Weick, 'Systematic Observational Methods', in ibid., p. 428.

13 Ernest Nagel, *The Structure of Science*, London: Routledge & Kegan Paul, 1961, p. 489.

14 See, for example, Johan Galtung, *Theory and Methods of Social Research*, London: Allen & Unwin, 1967, especially p. 121. Paul Siegel and Robert Hodge, 'A Causal Approach to the Study of Measurement Error', in Hubert and Ann Blalock (eds), *Methodology in Social Research*, New York: McGraw-Hill, 1971. Lee J. Cronback, *Essentials of Psychological Testing*, New York: Harper, 1949.

15 Weick, op. cit., p. 428.

16 Nagel, op. cit., p. 489.

17 John Madge, *The Origins of Scientific Sociology*, New York: Free Press, 1962, p. 120.

18 Julius Roth, 'Information and Control in Tuberculosis Hospitals', in Elliot Freidson (ed.), *The Hospital in Modern Society*, Chicago: Free Press, 1963, p. 294.

19 William J. Goode, 'Community within a Community: The Professions,' *American Sociological Review*, 22, 1957, p. 196.

20 Mary Goss, 'Patterns of Bureaucracy among Hospital Staff Physicians', in Freidson, op. cit., p. 176.

21 More than encouraging reliability, the signature seems to amount to a *claim* by the record-writer that he is reliable. Here the important point to notice is that, implicit in such a claim is a recognition that observer reliability *matters*. However, another issue is why the administration wants the observer to make a *claim*. We shall consider the signature again, from the viewpoint of its status as a claim, in the next chapter.

22 The staff are very much aware of the legal responsibility that goes with signing (or not signing) a record. They often advise each other about whether or not to sign certain entries. For example, an emergency room nurse said to an intern concerning a patient who could not be admitted for administrative reasons: 'You ought to put your name on the chart just to protect yourself; you saw him.'

23 A resident in the emergency room, for example, was asked to countersign an intern's write-up. After reading what the intern had written, he said, 'I won't sign that.' Instead, he and the intern discussed the case further.

24 Thus, instead of letting residents 'authenticate' their records,

interns will often ask the resident for advice before even writing their note.

25 As evidence of this point, careless errors often get repeated over and over in supposedly independent entries.

26 Op. cit., p. 28.

5 Completeness

1 See Merton, op. cit., pp. 199–200.

2 From an official memorandum of Mont Royal Hospital.

3 Ibid.

4 Ibid.

5 John McGibony, *Principles of Hospital Administration*, New York: Putnams, 1952, p. 468.

6 This is not to deny the point made in the last chapter that the signature is used by the bureaucrat as a device to encourage reliability. In the last chapter, we discussed the issue of why a signature would be relevant to a bureaucrat. Here the issue is why a signature would be irrelevant to a record-writer. Below, we discuss further aspects of the relevance of a signature to a bureaucrat. We suggest that the signature serves to make the record into an event.

7 Plato, *Crito*, in *The Dialogues of Plato*, trans. by B. Jowett, vol. 1, Oxford: Clarendon Press, 1953, p. 374.

8 Ibid.

9 Ibid., p. 384.

10 Ibid.

11 *The Dialogues of Plato*, vol. 2, p. 368.

12 Ibid.